Kitchen Storage

By the Editors of Sunset Books
and Sunset Magazine

*Special shelf for food processor or mixer swings up to
convenient work height (see page 31).*

Lane Publishing Co.
Menlo Park, California

Dishes ride on slide-out shelves for easy access (see page 31).

Book Editor
Don Vandervort

Coordinating Editor
Gregory J. Kaufman

Design
Roger Flanagan

Illustrations
Bill Oetinger

Thanks...

to the many architects, designers, and home owners who shared their ideas with us, especially Michael Goldberg, C.K.D., of The Kitchen Specialist; Stewart Fair at Kitchens by Stewart; Julie Ball of Great Kitchens at Boucher's; Del Brandstrom of The Refacers, Inc.; Rick Sambol of Kitchen Consultants; California Kitchens; Stacks & Stacks; and Crate & Barrel.

We extend special thanks to Phyllis Elving for her careful editing of the manuscript.

Cover: Designed for efficiency, remodeled kitchen features cooking island, generous counter space, and abundant storage. Design: Allen Sayles, Architectural Kitchens & Baths. Cover design by Susan Bryant. Photography by Stephen Marley.

Photographers: Glenn Christiansen: 8, 9 bottom, 11 top, 19 bottom, 29 bottom left; Peter Christiansen: 37 top left and right; Stephen Cridland: 18 top; Renee Lynn: 15 bottom left and right, 24 top, 42, 43, 48; Jack McDowell: 1, 2, 3, 17 top, 21 right, 23 top, 27 left, 29 top left, 31 top left and bottom right, 32 right, 33 top and bottom right, 34, 36, 37 bottom left; Stephen Marley: 15 top, 18 bottom, 20, 21 left, 22, 31 top right, 44 left and bottom right, 46; Don Normark: 9 top; Norman A. Plate: 7, 13, 16; Chad Slattery: 10 bottom, 40 bottom; Rob Super: 25, 33 bottom left, 40 top, 41 top left; Russ Widstrand: 4, 5, 10 top, 14 top, 17 bottom, 19 top, 27 right, 28, 30, 31 bottom left, 32 top and bottom left, 35, 37 bottom right, 38 left, 41 bottom left and center right, 44 top and center right; Tom Wyatt: 11 bottom, 12, 14 bottom, 23 bottom right, 24 bottom, 26, 29 top right, 38 right, 39.

Photo styling: JoAnn Masaoka Van Atta: 1, 4, 5, 11 bottom, 12 top, 15 bottom left and right, 17 bottom, 18 bottom, 23 bottom right, 24, 26, 27 bottom, 28, 29 top left, 30, 31 bottom right, 32 bottom left, 33 bottom right, 35, 38 left, 42, 43, 44 left, 46.

Editor, Sunset Books: Elizabeth L. Hogan

Second printing April 1990

Contents

Pivoting pull-out reclaims lost space in corner of base cabinets (see page 36).

The Organized Kitchen

Thanks to sky-high real estate values, two-income life-styles, and an influx of new technology, the kitchen has assumed a new identity in recent years. Today's kitchen is the hub of the household—a place of community where we gather with family and friends. And it is a dynamic workspace, filled with high-tech machines to dice onions, brew espresso, extrude pasta, extract juices, and handle scores of other chores.

To meet the challenge of its new identity, today's kitchen must be carefully planned. Filled with gear and yet open to the household and its guests, it needs to provide abundant storage. To maximize every valuable cubic inch of space and every valuable moment in our busy lives, that storage must be both space-efficient and easily accessible.

One thoughtfully organized kitchen is shown on these two pages. You'll find scores of other ideas in this book to inspire and aid you in transforming your own kitchen into an equally efficient workspace.

Essence of efficiency
Large storage island is just the beginning of this kitchen's efficiencies. Clutter-free, spacious, and organized for easy use, this kitchen was designed for a busy family. Kitchen design: Laurie Candelora.

Baking center and pantry

Generous drawers behind large doors provide capacious storage for foods. Pull-out counter is handy near microwave and ovens. Above ovens, trays and baking pans stay organized between vertical dividers.

Cabinet organizers

Custom oak spice shelves mount to inside of cabinet door. Below cabinet, tambour door rolls up to reveal food processor.

Full-feature island

Cutting board pulls out for chopping next to preparation sink. Large drawers below hold breads and cereals. Cabinets and drawers all around island offer abundant storage.

Hard-working shelves and drawers

Access to corner cabinet's full depth is made possible by corner carousel fitted to inside of angled double door. Drawers beneath cooktop hold pots, pans, and lids. Doors close to conceal drawers for neater kitchen lines, but they could be eliminated for quicker access.

Storage Components

Cabinets are a kitchen's key storage components. They create the personality of a kitchen and provide the structure for most of its organization and storage. For this reason—and because they represent the largest single investment in a new kitchen—it is important to study the many options available before purchasing new cabinets.

What materials do you prefer? Your choices include warm hardwoods, European-style laminates, painted veneers. Will you buy stock cabinets at the local lumberyard, order custom modular cabinets, or have cabinetry hand-crafted by a custom cabinetmaker? Your decisions will depend upon the look you want for your kitchen and how much money you're willing to spend to achieve that look.

Several other kitchen components supplement the storage provided by cabinets. Open shelving offers both visible display and quick access. Islands provide countertop space and centralized storage. Storage walls and pantries house paraphernalia and foods en masse. And carts roll about the kitchen, keeping frequently needed items within arm's length.

You'll find examples of typical cabinet options and ideas for other storage components throughout this chapter. For information on outfitting cabinets with hard-working hardware, see page 26. And for information on planning, selecting, and buying cabinets, see the Design Workbook beginning on page 46.

A harmony of kitchen elements
Cabinets, shelving, and islands or peninsulas are key storage elements contributing to a kitchen's appearance and efficiency. Sleek white laminate cabinets in this kitchen complement home's contemporary style. Custom elements include wine rack and, below, appliance storage area behind roll-up tambour door. Design: David Knox, Zephyr Architectural Partnership.

Cabinets: Design Choices

Basic building blocks of kitchen storage

Custom color

Bright red lacquered cabinets reach to ceiling; matching panels cover refrigerator. Lacquered finishes offer glossy elegance, but they're not for everyone—they are quite expensive and unforgiving of scratches and dents. Design: Robert Schatz, Plus Kitchens.

Kitchen curves

Undulating perimeter cabinets wrap around figure-eight island. Curves, which generally enhance price as well as appearance, are easiest to form with laminates. Architect: William P. Bruder. Cabinetmaker: Laurent Construction.

Craftsman's touch

Custom kitchen contains features you won't find in a stock-cabinet catalog. Cabinet faces have raised beaded panels, large-radius corners. Paneling also covers appliance faces, cabinet sides, sink soffit, and flared hood above cooktop. Design: Rob Boynton, Midland Cabinets.

Wood Cabinetry

Bringing nature's richness and warmth to the kitchen

Country fresh

Light-stained oak combines the warmth of wood with the pale tones characteristic of contemporary kitchens. Cabinets feature raised-bevel panel doors, large drawers beneath cooktop, and built-in microwave oven. Kitchen design: Kathy Grundhoffer. Cabinets: Kitchens by Stewart (Wood-Mode).

Rustic pine

Knotty-pine cabinets, owner-built from glass and blemished lumber, create a rustic mood. Glass doors display contents yet discourage dust. Chopping blocks set into gray-blue ceramic tile counter beside sink and cooktop take heavy use in food preparation. Design: Fred Spencer and Karen Brooks.

Sleek and contemporary

Even-toned custom wood cabinetry is of bleached and oiled vertical-grain clear fir. Countertops of white plastic laminate provide contrast. At the closed end of the U is a raised breakfast bar. Architect: Robert Anderson. Interior designer: Sheryl W. McKinsey.

Upscale elegance

Dark mahogany, marble, brass, and stainless steel distinguish this older home's kitchen. Matching custom panels mask refrigerator. Dark woods can express old-world warmth and character. Design: Osburn Design.

Laminate Cabinets

Crisp, clean lines and easy-care surfaces

Softened lines

Off-white laminate cabinets, typical of contemporary "Euro-style" kitchens, are durable and easy to clean. Generally a less-expensive choice than hardwoods, laminates lend themselves to curved surfaces. Architect: William B. Remick. Interior designer: Jane Howerton Interiors.

A study in black and white

Gleaming polished granite countertops reflect white-white cabinets in crisp, ultramodern kitchen. Though laminates are available in hundreds of colors and textures, white can be the most striking choice in the right setting. Rich slate tile floor enhances the contrast. Architect: Rob Wellington Quigley.

Warm gray

Cabinets and island of medium-gray laminate combine with deep purple tiles to convey richness, warmth, and comfort. Angled walls add interest at far end. Island doubles as counter and storage. Architect: Gary Gilbar.

Cabinet Variations

Unusual materials and slight twists expand your options

A place for plaster

Unusual? You bet! Though most of this kitchen's cabinet surfaces are laminates, the island and part of the wall that houses ovens have a plaster finish. These surfaces blend with the surrounding walls, complementing the contemporary Southwest theme. Design: Finnegan/Widstrand Company and City Cabinetmakers.

Best of both worlds

Combining wood and laminates can take advantage of both materials' benefits. Laminates on large surfaces are relatively inexpensive and easy to maintain. Using wood for trim or smaller surfaces adds a touch of natural warmth. Design: European Kitchens & Baths.

Popular alternative

Painted wood cabinets are an excellent, inexpensive alternative to hardwood and laminate cabinets. Walls and cabinets can match precisely; a color change is just a stroke of the brush away.

Face-lifting for a new look

Centerpiece of this kitchen remodel was refacing—rather than replacing—existing cabinets. Configuration of cabinets before remodel, left, suited owners' needs adequately, but resurfacing them with a whitewashed wood laminate gave a lighter, updated look—at considerably less cost than installing all new cabinetry. Design: Del Brandstrom, The Refacers, Inc.

Open Shelves

Simple, inexpensive—and indispensable—storage solutions

Quick access

Doors of upper cabinet fall short to allow open shelves, an ideal parking spot for frequently used dishware or kitchen paraphernalia. These basic frameless white cabinet boxes, typically made of painted or laminate fiberboard, have bleached wood doors— one of several style options. Bought knocked down, cabinets were assembled and installed by owner.

Cookbook storage, hidden lighting

Cookbooks and metal canisters stay out of the way but still within easy reach on this handy shelf. Fixtures mounted to underside of shelf provide light for baking counter below. Architects: Fisher-Friedman Associates.

Reference center

Open-shelf cabinet houses bound cooking magazines, cookbooks, and even a small television. This cabinet was manufactured to match the balance of the kitchen's cabinetry. Kitchen design: Kathy Grundhoffer. Cabinets: Kitchens by Stewart (Wood-Mode).

Hard-working Islands

Expanding kitchen counter space, stretching storage

Heart of the kitchen

Generously sized island adds to kitchen in two ways: by providing storage in its base and by offering abundant counter space, relieving storage needs elsewhere. Handsome Italian granite slab surface is both an excellent surface for pastry and candy making and a grand piece of horizontal art. Design: Don Atwood. Craftsperson: John Hall.

Multipurpose island

For on-the-go meals, cooking, and easy-access storage, island plays a major role in this kitchen. To accommodate normal chair height, counter steps down. Interior design: Ruth Livingston.

Preparation center

Broad counter, storage drawers, and small food-preparation sink make this island an activity hub. Cabinets, island, and countertop are all of white laminate. Architect: Martin Bernstein. Cabinetmakers: City Cabinetmakers.

For one or more chefs

Great for food preparation and display, generous island in expansive kitchen also houses a cooktop and numerous storage cabinets. Corners are angled to allow free traffic circulation. Architect: Kenneth Kurtzman, Kurtzman and Kodama, Inc. Interior decorator: Caryl Kurtzman.

Storage Walls

Floor-to-ceiling cabinets devoted to storage

Cupboards for dining gear

Everything from table leaves to coffee cups is kept in floor-to-ceiling cupboards along wall separating dining room from kitchen. Table leaves, folding chairs fit between blocks of wood nailed to top and bottom of cupboard compartments. Shelves fill in remaining space. Design: Pennington & Pennington.

Built-in storage

Recessed into dining area wall, shallow cupboards offer adjustable shelves for storing kitchen's overflow. Casseroles, tableware, baskets, and groceries hide behind tall doors. Antique cabinet at left houses more dishes and table linens. Interior designer: Joan Simon.

Flexible food cabinet

Sparkling white double doors swing open to reveal a flexible food storage system in frameless cabinet. Drawers are roomy enough for tall bottles of soda and a big basket brimming with oranges. Shelves adjust on metal tracks to accommodate jumbo-size food packages. Architects: Fisher-Friedman Associates.

A whole wall of storage

The beauty of these cabinets lies in their natural finish, clean lines, and almost unlimited storage capacity. Spacious shelves behind cabinet doors hold packaged foods, canned goods, and dishes; vented tip-out bins are filled with fruits and vegetables. Large baskets and crockery fit in space between cabinets and ceiling. Architect: Robert C. Peterson.

Walk-in Pantries

Satellite rooms lead the race for space

Joint venture in wine and food storage

Walk-in pantry features wine "cellar" on far wall and a cooler to keep wines at proper temperature. Pantry shelves are fixed at various heights. Ladder brings top shelves within reach. Design: Gordon Grover.

This one has it all

Walk-in pantry (at left) holds everything but the kitchen sink. Shelves on walls adjust to accommodate kitchen equipment of different heights; hooks hold molds and small cooking utensils. Packaged foods and canned goods fit in single rows on shallow door shelves. Especially convenient are counter for preparing food and storing appliances, undershelf baskets for fruits and vegetables, and storage place for stool. Architects: Sortun-Vos.

Hidden mini-pantry

Behind sliding louvered doors, a roomy pantry houses food, appliances, and other kitchen gear. Pantry interior is lined with open shelving. Architect: Peter C. Rodi, Designbank.

Kitchen Carts

Counter space and storage on the move

Ready-made rolling storage

Coated-wire cart topped with laminate work surface glides across the kitchen for easy table-setting. Pull-out baskets and hardware are sturdy enough to allow storage of dishes as well as table linens; such commercially available carts are adaptable to all sorts of kitchen storage needs.

Stowaway

Compact baking center comes out of hiding, rolls to any part of the kitchen, then tucks away neatly in a counter end when work is done. The marble top is great for pastry and candy making; metal-lined tilt-out bins below hold flour and sugar. Baking gear stores in the lowest compartment. Architect: William B. Remick.

Roll-around multipurpose cart

For flower arranging— or any other purpose— this cart rolls out from underneath counter to become a work island. Shelves and drawers provide storage for infrequently used items. Design: Plus Kitchens.

More than a butcher block

Beneath lavish array of gleaming cookware is a butcher block table fitted with casters. Modified to include a lift-out metal bin with cover, sliding blade-storage tray, wire basket, and even towel pegs, island moves from one kitchen work center to another. For a home where children are present, knives and food processor blades would be best kept elsewhere. Architect: Peter W. Behn.

Outfitting Cabinetry

When planning your kitchen's storage scheme, imagine your cabinets as empty boxes, perched on the floor or mounted on the wall. Then consider how you might outfit these boxes to provide the most efficient and accessible storage for your kitchen. Starting with a "blank slate" is often the best way to see your kitchen's storage potential.

Numerous accessories can be used to extend the usefulness of cabinetry: doors in several styles, fixed and movable shelves, drawers and baskets, carousels and lazy Susans, specialty pull-outs, space-saving racks, and more. This chapter illustrates some of your choices.

Though you can buy accessories such as shelf supports, drawer glides, and space-saving racks at home-improvement stores, many specialty pull-outs and organizers are sold only to cabinet-makers, manufacturers, and dealers. If you're ordering new cabinets, you can page through catalogs that show options. If you're updating your existing cabinetry, ask dealers or cabinetmakers whether they can order specialty hardware for you.

Supercenter

Mild-mannered cabinets (above) conceal super powers of storage and organization (right). Built for a serious pastry cook, this baking center features everything needed in one well-thought-out unit. The granite top is both pastry slab and landing place for hot dishes; beneath it, a bread board and oven coexist with a wealth of storage that leaves no space untapped. Design: Carlene Anderson, CKD.

Pull-out pantry

Gliding smoothly on heavy-duty hardware, one of a pair of birch and alder pull-out pantries keeps food storage centralized in the middle of the kitchen. Dividers above ovens keep cooking and serving trays organized. Architect: Michael D. Moyer, The Architectural Design Group.

Dynamic duo

Small drawer front drops down to reveal pull-out chopping block. Beneath it, waste bin slides out when you pull open cabinet door. These features are typical of specialty hardware available through cabinet dealers. Cabinets: Wood-Mode.

Cabinet Doors

Options that affect your kitchen's form and function

Potpourri of doors

Cabinets at left are outfitted with three different styles of doors. Tambour door retracts into curved corner cabinet, glass doors display crystal and glassware, and raised-bevel panel doors cover everything else. Above, round-cornered cabinet, part of the same custom modular system, has door shaped to flow with the curve. Cabinets: Wood-Mode.

Roll-top appliance nooks

Ideal for appliance garages at countertop level, tambour doors stay out of the way when open. Be sure tambours are counterbalanced properly so they don't drop shut when you let go.

Disappearing doors

Doors can be mounted on sliding hinges so they pivot open, then slide into cabinet to remain out of the way. Side-mounted doors work well for television cabinet, as shown here. Doors can be top-mounted, too—an excellent solution for countertop appliance cabinets. Architect: William B. Remick.

Glass sliders

Bridge of black laminate cabinets spans concrete island. Glass doors keep glassware in view but dust-free. Instead of swinging out into the kitchen where they might cause an accident, these doors slide in grooves. Architect: Ted Tokio Tanaka.

Interior Shelves

The cabinet's most basic organizers—some typical choices

Standard adjusments

Adjustable shelves in manufactured cabinets typically rest on metal pins inserted into holes drilled in cabinet sides. This system is both adjustable and inconspicuous.

Tracks and clips

Screwed to cabinet's inner walls, track-and-clip system is highly adjustable. For a do-it-yourselfer, mounting tracks is much easier than aligning and drilling hundreds of holes for shelf pins.

See-through shelves

An elegant alternative to standard shelving, glass shelves are an excellent choice for display case or for high, light-duty shelves where you may want to identify contents from below.

Modified shelving

Particleboard shelves, edged with wood trim, are notched to receive cabinet's door-mounted spice rack when door closes. Shelves sit on dowel pegs pushed into holes drilled in groups of four.

Pull-out shelves for amplified access

Shelves mounted with drawer glides are a popular option in today's kitchen. Particularly in base cabinets, pull-out shelves allow you to reach items at very back quickly and easily. Architect: Woodward Dike.

Shelves or shallow drawers?

Concealed behind cabinet door, stack of shallow drawer/shelves keeps placemats organized. Low fronts leave contents highly visible and serve as drawer pulls. Architect: Bo-Ivar Nyquist.

Rising to the occasion

Spring-up shelf serves as storage area when down, work surface when up. Though hardware is relatively expensive, such a shelf is very handy for food processor or heavy mixer and can be adapted to most cabinets.

Adjustable pull-out

Special mounting tracks and brackets make this drawer-style shelf adjustable in height. Trade-off is loss of about 3 inches in shelf's width to accommodate hardware.

Drawers

Convenient, full-access storage solutions

Drawers galore

Long bank of drawers serves as primary storage in this kitchen. Drawers are efficient containers that offer full access to contents. Custom drawers like these are expensive; stock drawers, available in standard sizes at building supply centers, are more economical and can be adapted to fit most cabinetry—though often with some loss of storage space. Design: Pat Larin Interiors and City Cabinetmakers.

Drawers and more

Drawers come in all shapes and sizes. Cabinet door next to top oven is actually front of four-shelf drawer unit. Bottom cabinet houses two more drawers. Both units provide quick access to food and easily visible storage. Architect: Michael D. Moyer, The Architectural Design Group. Interior designer: Joan Simon.

Large-scale drawers

Beneath cooktop, wide drawers are sized to fit contents— cutlery and utensils on top, pots and pans below. Wide drawers require sturdy, heavy-duty glides and dual drawer pulls.

Touring a designer's kitchen

Bank of drawers (above) proves more efficient than regular cabinets with shelves. Two drawers are sized to hold standard boxes and metal container for flour. Carousel trays provide access to corner storage. Below sink (above right), large roll-out drawers disclose a trash can and cleaning supplies. Drawer beneath cooktop (right) holds pots; lids rest in a vertically divided drawer below. Jars in spice drawer are tilted for easy access. Design: Carlene Anderson, CKD.

Coated-wire baskets

Easily visible through coated wire, dishes can be removed from both sides of two-way cabinet. Placemats and napkins lie flat in adjacent drawers. Baskets are often a less-expensive alternative to drawers and are better for storing foods that require ventilation— such as potatoes and onions. Architect: Gilbert Oliver. Interior designer: Nancy Brown, ASID.

Drawer Organizers

Keeping contents orderly and easy to find

For the ardent cook

An army of knives stands at the ready, sheathed in a series of knife blocks set in deep, full-extension drawer. On one flank, slanted racks in shallow drawers keep entire inventory of spices visible. In a home where children live or visit, child-safety latches should be added to knife drawer (see page 44). Design: Gordon Grover.

Three typical organizers

Most cabinet manufacturers offer drawer organizers as options. Here are three examples. At top left is a plastic flatware tray, exactly fitted to the drawer. Above, a wooden knife block organizes miscellaneous cutlery in shallow drawer. At left, spices rest on tiered, angled drawer divider. Cabinets: Wood-Mode.

Carousels & Lazy Susans

Hardware for reclaiming lost and hard-to-reach cabinet space

Semicircular swing-outs

Making the most of space that would otherwise be lost in a "blind" corner, coated wire shelves swing open, then pull out to provide complete access to contents. Kitchen design: Bob Easton Design Associates.

Cabinet roundabout

Difficult corner cabinet can be handled with an L-shaped door that opens both sides of corner. Built-in lazy Susan pivots for complete access. Raised edges on shelves prevent spills. Architect: Ron Yeo.

Pivoting appliance garage

Tiled, 10-foot-long island terminates at low wall where appliance garage swings out of semicircular storage unit separating kitchen counter from dining area. Architect: Craig Roland, Roland/Miller/Associates.

Upper-cabinet lazy Susan

L-shaped door pivots into corner cabinet to reveal three attached rounded shelves that maximize use of corner's depth. This, like other carousels and lazy Susans, is an option available from manufacturers.

Floor-to-ceiling lazy Susan

Taking a good idea to its logical conclusion, corner lazy Susan measures 12 feet from top to bottom. Three sections, reached through separate doors, turn independently of one another. Each ¾-inch plywood tray measures 36 inches in diameter and has an aluminum lip. Middle section stores most-used equipment, bottom section is for less-used items, and top—reached via ladder— is for kitchen gear that's seldom needed. Architect: William B. Remick.

Cabinet Pantries

High-density food storage in the center of your kitchen

Generous food drawers

Hidden behind tall cabinet doors, five large oak drawers mounted on heavy-duty guides are filled to capacity with food. Shortened drawer fronts allow a quick scan of contents. Of all cabinet pantry options, drawers give you the most high-density storage for your money. Kitchen design: Kathy Grundhoffer. Cabinets: Kitchens by Stewart (Wood-Mode).

Narrow-and-wide pantry

Tall doors open to reveal a shallow pantry that divides available depth between doors and cabinet. Most goods are displayed in single ranks for simple selection and inventory. Architect: Hiro Morimoto/Atelier Architects.

Pull-out rack

When space is deep and narrow, pull-out rack on heavy-duty rollers offers effective storage for cans, bottles, and boxes. Architect: Steven Goldstein.

Fold-up pantry system

Unfolding like a child's puzzle, this pantry makes maximum use of standard cabinet dimensions. Door-mounted shelves, two-sided swing-out shelves, and more shelves at the back of the cabinet ensure access to every bit of space. Similar pantries are available through cabinet manufacturers. Design: Sarah Lee Roberts.

Specialty Accessories

Stretch your kitchen's usefulness with specialized fittings

The no-office office

At one end of contemporary kitchen, typewriter swings out and up from base cabinet. Files hang in special file "drawer" in cabinet at right; phone sits on counter. When not in use, this minimal home office completely disappears into cabinetry. Architect: Gilbert Oliver.

Instant table

Disguised as part of the cabinetry, tabletop pulls out of base cabinet. You can buy similar tables that, when fully extended, will seat up to five people.

Concealed laundry center

Sophisticated European fir cabinetry with black plastic laminate counters hides a pull-out ironing board and, in adjacent tall cabinet, a washer and dryer. Architect: Gilbert Oliver. Interior designer: Nancy Brown, ASID.

Wrinkle-free linens

Simple rack, built like a bottomless drawer with large dowels running from front to back, keeps table linens suspended in cabinet. Design: Wood-Mode.

Cleanup accessories

Beneath the kitchen sink, wire rack with adjustable shelves pulls out for easy access to cleaning supplies. When you open right-hand door, lid automatically lifts as trash can pivots out. Slim space in front of sink—normally wasted—holds narrow metal tray for sponges and scrubbers. Such accessories are available for many manufactured cabinet systems.

Space Extenders

Store-bought racks and holders that maximize storage

Shelving maximizers

Dinnerware, cups, and mugs stack on and hang from coated-wire shelf organizers. Several styles are available; shown here are a combination mug rack/shelf, a cup stacker, a shelf organizer for dinnerware and cups, and a shelf doubler.

Hanging shelves

Simple coated-wire hanging shelves slide onto existing shelving to reclaim lost space. Those shown here store placemats and napkins, adding much-needed shelf space quickly and inexpensively.

Undercabinet space-savers

Space beneath upper cabinets is maximized with specialty racks that store knives and stemware. You can buy similar racks to hold spices or cookbooks. Cabinet-mounted can openers, coffee makers, and other small appliances provide another way to take advantage of undercabinet space.

Wire utility racks

For kitchen garbage bags or miscellaneous items, you can mount coated-wire racks to cabinet walls or doors. Door mounted rack holds folded grocery bags as well as garbage sack.

Organizers for pans and lids

Avoid jumbled pans and lids by filing them in wire organizers that sit on cabinet shelves or pull-outs. These inexpensive racks, and a potpourri of others similar to them, are available at home improvement centers.

Safety Hardware

Where small children are present, remember to childproof

Childproof latch

Spring-loaded latch screws easily onto doors or drawers. When door closes, latch hooks to underside of cabinet stile, allowing door to open only far enough for adult finger pressure to release it.

Padlock for doors

Where cabinet knobs or pulls pair up, simple plastic lock—similar to a bicycle padlock—secures them together. An adult presses plastic button to release lock.

Handy extinguisher

Be prepared for fire: mount a fire extinguisher near kitchen's exit, above small children's reach and at least 6 feet from kitchen range.

Child-safe cooking area

Wire corral (from a children's store), stuck to countertop with suction cups, keeps small fingers from reaching pots or burners. Pot handles are turned inward to prevent spills. Wall-mounted rack hangs utensils well out of reach. Plastic plugs seal off unused electrical outlets; latches lock doors shut. Design: Lizette Wilbur.

Complete Kitchen Safety

More often than not, the kitchen is the heart of the home, a place where both adults and children spend much of their time. Because it is essentially a work center, filled with machines, utensils, appliances, and other potentially dangerous tools, this is where accidents are most likely to occur. Small children are particularly susceptible; more children's lives are lost in home accidents than in all childhood diseases combined.

The following are a few important steps you can take to help ensure your family's safety in the kitchen. But be aware that childproofing requires a comprehensive approach. Children, in their boundless curiosity, inevitably will find the few hazards left unprotected. For more detailed information on making your entire home and yard safe for small children, see the Sunset book *Making Your Home Child-Safe.*

General Safety

Whether or not you have small children, consider taking these important precautions:

■ Install a smoke detector between the kitchen and living areas, and keep a Class A-B-C fire extinguisher handy. If a small fire starts, first remove everyone from danger; then use the extinguisher. But if a fire is out of control, stop using the extinguisher and get everyone out of the house.

■ Reduce fire potential by storing flammables away from heat. Clean the entire cooking area frequently; grease buildup can be dangerous, yet it often goes unnoticed on concealed surfaces.

A grease fire in a cooking pan on the stovetop is extinguished by placing a lid over the pan and turning off the heat. Lack of oxygen snuffs out the fire. *Never try to put out a grease fire with water.* To put out an oven fire, just shut the oven door and turn off the heat.

■ At the kitchen range, loose sleeves can catch fire easily; so can dishtowels used as pot holders. When cooking, wear trim-fitting clothes and use pot holders designed for the purpose.

■ Natural and LP gas are scented to alert you to leaks. For a major leak or service interruption, evacuate the house, turn off the main gas valve, and immediately call your utility company from a telephone outside your house. For minor leaking caused by a blown-out pilot, ventilate the room thoroughly. Then relight the pilot according to the manufacturer's instructions, or call your utility company.

Sparks can ignite gas— don't turn on electric switches or appliances if you suspect a leak.

■ To avoid carbon monoxide and nitrogen dioxide poisoning, make sure that your gas range has a hood fan or other exhaust fan that vents fumes to the outdoors. Never use a gas oven to heat your rooms, and never cook with charcoal indoors.

■ Use properly grounded outlets with adequate fuses or properly-sized circuit breakers. Don't overload circuits (hot plugs are a warning sign). Avoid outlet "extenders," or "cube taps" and extension cords.

■ Unplug appliances immediately after use. Keep appliances away from water; never touch water while you're using them. Always unplug appliances for cleaning or repairs.

If You Have Small Children...

When there are young children in the household, you should take several basic steps to minimize the possibility of their being injured in your kitchen.

■ Keep baby out from underfoot when working in the kitchen. A playpen or feeding table set a safe distance from the range and other hazards protects baby while allowing companionship with the cook.

■ Pick up and store anything that might be hazardous to your baby— small, sharp, breakable, or poisonous objects.

■ Remove dangerous items from any cabinets within your child's reach. In most kitchens, the place to start is under the sink. Move frequently used supplies, such as dishwasher detergent, to an upper cabinet with an easy-access latch (see photos on facing page). Put garbage in a container with a hard-to-open lid— or store it under the sink and install a child-resistant latch on that door.

Most kitchen cleansers and related chemicals are packaged in bright containers that may make them look edible or drinkable to a small, curious child. Don't leave any of these products within reach. And never store them in containers that originally held food or drink, such as soft-drink bottles.

Move liquor to a cabinet with a child-resistant latch or to an out-of-reach spot. Keep knives safely beyond your child's reach— yet convenient to you, so that you'll be sure to put them away again after use.

■ Don't let electrical cords dangle over countertop edges where they might be pulled. Put away all kitchen utensils after use. Small appliances should be unplugged when not in use and stored out of reach. Always remove and put away any sharp blades.

Design Workbook

Imagining your dream kitchen isn't enough. You want to make it *happen*. As anyone who has ever experienced a remodel will tell you, making the leap from fantasy to reality takes work.

Your first task—whether you're modifying your existing kitchen or building a new one— is to begin planning. Cabinets, appliances, counters, islands, pantries, plumbing, wiring—a variety of elements must be orchestrated carefully to create a kitchen that truly meets your family's needs.

Start with the main ingredient—the storage— and then work out the other components. On the facing page, you'll find some guidelines for basic kitchen planning. Turn to pages 48-53 for information on selecting and buying cabinets. For the complete story on planning and designing your kitchen, see the Sunset book *Kitchen Planning & Remodeling*.

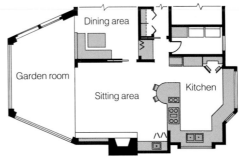

Planning pays off

Thoughtful kitchen design is keyed to family's living patterns. Layout creates comfortable work areas and small table for quick breakfasts; cabinetry provides storage that's efficient and accessible yet inconspicuous. Plan (above) shows how kitchen relates to the part of the home where family spends most of their time. Architect: Donald King Loomis. Interior designer: Ruth Livingston.

About Kitchen Planning

A few important fundamentals

Whether you're hiring a professional designer to plan your kitchen or doing the planning yourself, it's a good idea to consider a few basic design concepts in the early stages. This will help you to identify your needs and get a handle on what work will be involved.

If the scope of your project calls for it, work with a professional designer. Architects, interior designers, kitchen designers, and some kitchen showroom salespeople are experienced in designing kitchens; look under "Kitchen Cabinets" in your phone book. Cabinetmakers also often provide a design service when custom-building cabinets. Whomever you choose, be sure they are qualified in this specialized field. Ask for references, and visit actual installations they have designed. See page 51 for more about getting help.

Start your planning by taking graph paper and a tape measure in hand and drawing a basic floor plan of your existing kitchen, measuring as exactly as possible (within ⅛ inch). Include dimensions of walls, windows, and doors; indicate placement of existing cabinets, appliances, and lights. You'll need this floor plan for developing and communicating your ideas.

Though there is no formula for "the ideal kitchen," the guidelines discussed on this page have proven to be important in creating efficient, workable spaces.

Take Inventory

To determine the best storage for your kitchen's contents, first take an inventory of everything stored in your cabinets now. Then consider what else you would store if your kitchen were larger or more efficient. List all the various items, giving a rough idea of the space requirement for each. Then, as you develop kitchen plans, assign each item a space.

Divide & Conquer

When you're planning your kitchen, it's helpful to divide the room according to the functions to be performed in each different area. Though kitchen spaces are interrelated, it's easiest to examine their design elements separately.

Four centers are basic to most kitchens: sink, cooking, refrigerator, and preparation. In addition, you may want to include a planning/work center or possibly an entertaining center with a second sink.

Sink center. Besides the obvious—a sink—this center may include a dishwasher, garbage disposer, and trash compactor, as well as cabinets and drawers. This is where food is rinsed and trimmed, wastes and recyclables are disposed of, dishes are washed and stored.

Provide storage space for chopping board, food preparation utensils, trash, and dishwashing and cleaning supplies. Stow dishes and glassware as close as possible to the dishwasher for easy unloading.

Cooking center. The range—or separate cooktop and oven—is the focus of a cooking center, which may also include a microwave or convection oven and various electric cooking appliances. You may have more than one cooking center; the cooktop is handy to have central in the kitchen, but ovens may be more out of the way.

Near the appropriate appliances, store pots and pans, roasting racks, cooky sheets, and muffin tins. Keep cooking utensils and pot holders within easy reach.

Refrigerator center. This center may consist of not only a refrigerator and several cabinets, but perhaps also a floor-to-ceiling pantry wedged between refrigerator and adjacent wall. If you store nonperishable food items near the refrigerator, putting groceries away is a snap. Tuck plastic wrap, foil, plastic bags, and freezer containers into a nearby drawer or cabinet.

Preparation center. If you have enough room, design a food preparation center with storage for small appliances—food processor, toaster, mixer, and electric can opener, for example. Locating this center near the refrigerator and/or sink simplifies mixing and serving chores. Keep cookbooks and recipe boxes nearby. Store canisters, mixing bowls, and small utensils close at hand, and you'll waste little motion preparing meals.

Consider Layout

Locate the major appliances—sink, range or cooktop, and refrigerator—so that the resulting work triangle is out of the traffic pattern. For efficiency, position these three elements so that the distance between any two of them (measured from center front to center front) is at least 4 feet but no more than 9 feet. Keep the sum of the triangle sides to less than 26 feet.

Allow sufficient space between counters and around eating areas. You'll need at least 48 inches between opposite work counters; between a counter and an island, 36 inches may be ample. If two or more people are likely to share the kitchen, you may want to expand these dimensions. Be sure to plan adequate counter space for preparing foods, unloading groceries, processing dirty dishes, setting out dinner, and so forth.

Place tall appliances or cabinets on the ends of a run of counter to avoid interrupting the work flow. Allow clearance for swinging cabinet doors and front-opening appliances (for example, you'll need 20 inches in front of a dishwasher for loading).

Selecting Your Cabinets

Understanding what's available and figuring your needs

Professional help

In showroom of sample kitchens, professional designer demonstrates features of faceframe cabinet door. Kitchen cabinet showrooms are the best places to view a variety of styles; often they offer complete design services.

You've planned, figured, drawn, and considered. Now it's time to get down to business. You must select and order your new cabinets. Why is making a decision so difficult?

Cabinets have a greater impact on a kitchen's design than any other element. You know you'll live with your decision on a daily basis for years to come. And there are *so many* styles to consider.

To make the decision easier, you need to arm yourself with some basic knowledge. The information on these pages will show you the two ways all cabinets are constructed and the three possible ways you can buy cabinets. Basic cabinet units can be modified and organized in many different ways to create a functional kitchen. Your own particular space and budgetary considerations will help determine what's best for you.

Traditional or European-style?

One of the first choices to make is between traditional "faceframe" cabinets or European-style frameless cabinetry. As a rule, manufacturers specialize in one style or the other (though some manufacturers make both).

Faceframe cabinets. Until recently, traditional American cabinetmakers have masked the raw front edges of each cabinet box with a 1 by 2 "faceframe." Doors and drawers in such a cabinet fit in one of three ways: flush; partially inset, with a notch; or completely overlaying the frame. These are referred to as "flush," "offset," and "overlay," respectively.

Because the frame covers the edge, thin or low-quality panels or wood can be used in the sides of faceframe cabinets (thus reducing price). But the frame takes up space; it reduces the size of the opening, so drawers or slide-out accessories must be significantly smaller than the cabinet's width. In addition, typical door hinges for faceframe cabinets are visible from the front.

European-style frameless cabinets. Europeans, whose kitchens are often so tiny that all space counts, have been making "frameless" cabinets for years. Recently, American manufacturers have begun manufacturing these modular cabinets because of the system's popularity.

On frameless cabinets, a simple narrow trim strip covers raw panel edges, which butt directly against each other. All hardware (for doors, drawers, or accessories) mounts directly to the interior sides of the boxes; hinges are almost always invisible from the outside. Doors and drawers usually fit to within ¼ inch of each other, revealing little of the trim. Interior components— such as drawers— can be sized practically to the full interior dimension of the box.

Thanks to absolute standardization of every component, frameless cabinets are unsurpassed in versatility. Precise columns of holes are drilled on the inside faces. These holes are generally in the same places, no matter whose cabinets you buy, and components plug right into them.

The terms "system 32" and "32-millimeter" refer to the basic matrix of all these cabinets: all the holes, hinge fittings, cabinet joints, and mounts are set 32 millimeters apart.

Another big difference: frameless cabinets typically have a separate toe-space pedestal, or plinth. This allows you to set counter heights specifically to your liking, stack base units, or make use of space at floor level.

Stock, Custom, or Custom Modular?

Cabinets are manufactured and sold three different ways. The type you choose will affect the cost, appearance, and workability of your kitchen.

Stock cabinets. Buy your kitchen "off the shelf" and save— if you're careful. Mass-produced standard-size cabinets are the least expensive option, and they can be an excellent choice if you clearly understand the cabinetry you need for your kitchen. As the name implies, the range of sizes is limited.

Even so, you can always specify door styles, which direction doors swing, and whether side panels are finished. And you can often get options and add-ons such as breadboards, sliding shelves, and special corner units. Most stock systems also have cabinets that can be ordered for peninsulas or islands— with doors or drawers on both sides, and appropriate toes paces, trim, and finishes.

You may find stock lines heavily discounted at some home centers. But buying such cabinets can be a lot like doing your own taxes: no one really volunteers much information that will save you money or clarify your options— and if you make a mistake or get bad advice (even from a salesperson), you're the one who's liable. Knowledgeable people who can help you select stock cabinets tend to be the exception, not the rule.

Custom cabinets. Many people still have a cabinetmaker come to their house and measure, then return to the cabinet shop and build custom frame carcasses, drawers, and doors.

Custom cabinet shops can match old cabinets, size truly oddball configurations, and accommodate complexities that can't be handled with stock or modular cabinets. Such jobs generally cost considerably more than medium-line stock or modular cabinets.

Many cabinet shops take advantage of stock parts to streamline work and keep prices down. They buy door and drawer fronts from the same companies who make them for stock manufacturers. And cabinetmakers are using the same fine hardware (usually German) and tools (multiple-bit drills, metric hinge setters, and precise panel saws) developed for modular systems.

Some cabinet shops specialize in refacing existing kitchen cabinets. This can be an excellent, less-expensive choice than replacing the entire cabinet system, with results that look essentially the same as if you had done just that. Companies that will reface your existing cabinets also often buy mass-produced parts for the job.

Custom modular cabinets. Between stock and custom-made cabinetry are "custom modular cabinets" or "custom systems." Custom modular cabinets can

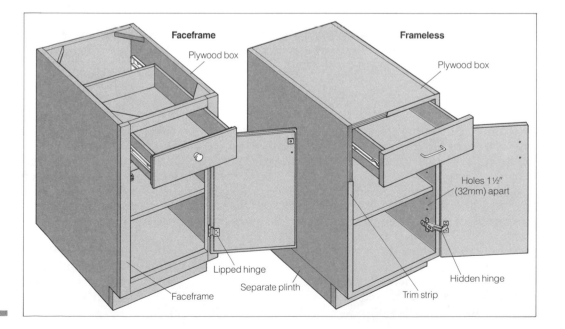

Traditional and European cabinets

Traditional faceframe cabinet (near right) has a wooden frame that covers the cabinet's front edges. European-style frameless cabinet (far right) eliminates frame— a simpler, more flexible system that takes better advantage of space.

Faceframe
Plywood box
Frameless
Plywood box
Holes 1½" (32mm) apart
Lipped hinge
Separate plinth
Faceframe
Hidden hinge
Trim strip

Comparing Cabinets

	STOCK	CUSTOM	CUSTOM MODULAR
Where to buy	Lumberyards, home improvement centers, appliance stores, some showrooms (most stock is made in this country).	Few shops have showrooms; most show pictures of completed jobs. Be safe; visit not only the shop but some installations, too.	If you know a brand name, check the yellow pages. These cabinets are mainly showroom items, but some are found in stock locations and department stores.
Who designs	You should, because the clerk helping you order may know less about cabinet options than you do. Don't order if you're at all unsure.	You; your architect, builder, or kitchen designer; or the maker (but be careful; cabinetmakers aren't necessarily designers).	The better (and more expensive) the line, the more help you get. Top-of-the-line suppliers design your whole kitchen; you just pick the style and write the check.
Cost range	Less than the other two choices, but you'll still swallow hard when you see the total. Look for heavy discounts at home centers, but pay attention to quality and craftsmanship.	Very wide; depends, as with factory-made boxes, on materials, finishes, craftsmanship, and options you choose.	A basic box can cost about what stock does, but each desirable modification or upgrade in door and drawer finishes boosts the cost considerably.
Options available	Only options may be door styles, hardware, and which way doors swing—but check the catalog; some lines offer a surprising range.	You can often—but not always—get the same options and European-made hardware that go in custom modular cabinets.	Most lines offer choices galore—including variations in basic sizes and options for corner spaces. Check showrooms and study catalogs.
Materials used	Cheaper lines may use doors of mismatched or lower-quality woods, composite, or thinner laminates that photo-simulate wood.	Anything you specify, but see samples. Methods vary by cabinetmaker; look at door and drawer hardware in a finished kitchen.	Factory-applied laminates and catalyzed varnishes are usually high quality and durable. Medium-density fiberboard is superior alternative for nonshowing wood.
Delivery time	You may be able to pick up cabinets at a warehouse the same day you order. Wait is generally (but not always) shorter than for other types.	Figure five weeks or longer, depending on job complexity, material and hardware availability, number of drawers, finishes.	Five to eight weeks is typical, whether cabinets are American or imported, but don't be surprised if they take up to six months. Order as soon as you know what you want.
Installation & service	Depends on where you buy; supplier may recommend a contractor. Otherwise, you install yourself. Service is virtually nonexistent.	In most cases, the maker installs. Buy from an established shop and you should have no trouble getting service if anything doesn't work right.	Better lines are sold at a price that includes installation and warranty (one of the reasons price is higher). Some cabinets are virtually guaranteed for life.
Other considerations	You often pay in full up front, giving you little recourse if cabinets are shipped wrong. Be sure order is absolutely correct and complete.	Make sure the bid you accept is complete—not just a basic cost-per-foot or cost-per-box charge.	With some manufacturers, if cabinets are wrong, you'll wait as long for the right parts to arrive as you did in the first place. Check.

offer the best of both worlds. They are manufactured, but they are of a higher grade and offer more design flexiblity than stock cabinets. Not surprisingly, they cost more, too.

Custom systems offer a wide range of sizes, with many options within each size. A good modular shop can do all but truly custom work, using its own components to build a kitchen from finished units. By modifying modular components, you come close to custom cabinetry.

You can change practically everything on these basic modules: add sliding shelves; replace doors with drawers; set a matching hood unit over the stove; add wire baskets, flour bins, appliance garages, and pull-out pantries.

The key to the versatility of these systems is that, if necessary, basic dimensions can be modified to fit virtually any kitchen configuration. Heights, widths, and depths can be changed so that you can adjust units to practically any size.

Though frameless modular cabinets (see pages 48-49) are sized metrically (standard cabinet depth is 60 centimeters— about 24 inches), virtually all lines are now sized for American appliances. And sizes break into about 3-inch increments, with custom dimensions available.

What Options Are Available?

Perhaps more options exist for corners than for any other kitchen cabinet space. If you don't use specially designed cabinets in corners, you'll lose a lot of valuable space. The simplest corner butts one cabinet against another, providing inconvenient access to the corner. Better options include diagonal units with a larger door, double-door units that provide full access to the L-shaped space, and lazy Susans or other slide-out accessories that bring items from the back up to the front.

Many hardware options are available to add to the versatility of kitchen cabinets. You'll find examples throughout this book, particularly on pages 26-41.

Judging Quality

To determine quality in cabinetry, look closely at the drawers; they take more of a beating than any other part of the cabinet. Compare drawers in several lines of cabinets, examining the joinery of each, and you'll see differences.

Drawer guides and cabinet hinges are the critical hardware elements. Check for adjustability of both; you should be able to reset and fine-tune them with the cabinets in place. Some frameless cabinets also have adjustable mounting hardware, so you can relevel them even after they've been hung on the wall. Determine whether drawer glides allow full or only partial extension of drawers. Check to see that doors and drawers align properly.

Getting Help

The cabinets are only part of the puzzle. When you buy cabinets, some of what you're paying for is varying degrees of help with kitchen design.

A kitchen designer will help you figure out how you'll use your kitchen. Some retailers will have you fill out a questionnaire to help determine what's wrong with your current kitchen, how often you do any specialty cooking, whether your guests always end up in the kitchen, whether you buy food in bulk, and other clues in reaching a design solution.

A showroom with many lines of cabinets will give you a better idea of what you want—and the designer a sense of what you're after. Pick a look, and then shop for it; compare features, craftsmanship, and cost. If you're serious about buying, make an appointment with a showroom (try to make it for a time when the place won't be too busy). Some showrooms will also carry the other kitchen components you'll need, such as counters, appliances, sinks, and fixtures.

Some designers may represent a particular line of cabinets, so shop around to get an idea of what's available. Once you become serious, be sure that you like the particular line of cabinets a showroom designer handles.

Your current floor plan is the best aid you can offer a designer (see page 47). Some staff designers in showrooms will do the new cabinet plan for you, applying the charge against the purchase price of cabinets. In fact, some retailers offer a complete kitchen planning service when you buy their cabinets. Some showrooms even use computer renderings to help customers visualize the finished kitchen— and prices for different cabinet configurations are just a keystroke away.

Your budget will affect more than your choice of cabinets. Often you can pay less for some lines by shopping where design services aren't necessarily included. But keep in mind that as you step down in price, you must take on more and more responsibility yourself; *you* have to guarantee the accuracy of every step in the process.

Figuring Costs & Ordering

There are no figures under "Cost range" in the chart at left. Why? Because so many factors influence the final price. The kitchens shown in this book have cabinets that range from about $400 to more than $80,000.

The range of styles—and prices—makes buying cabinets much like buying a car. Like car makers, every manufacturer or cabinetmaker picks a market position, then offers various styles and options that jack up or bring down the price. If you're looking for the cabinet equivalent of "transportation," you can pay a lot less than someone looking for something sportier.

Know your budget. You'll quickly find out what kinds of cabinets you can afford. With your plan in hand, you can get a base price for standard cabinets relatively easily. But options will drastically alter the quote— so the same basic cabinet can end up costing a lot of different prices. Be sure to obtain quotes based on a fully specified room sketch listing the options desired in each cabinet.

Within each line of cabinets, basic costs are determined by the style of the doors and drawers. The basic frame carcass will be the same within a line no matter what door style you choose. Wood choices can also affect price.

In many showrooms, you can get a general idea of costs by asking dealers for the prices of components in sample kitchens. A good showroom has an advantage over most custom shops: you can see many of the possibilities set up in one place.

Even if you're buying manufactured cabinets, consider getting an estimate from a custom shop for comparison. Such a shop can match practically any style or can come up with a pattern or finish not available in a modular or stock line. A cabinetmaker will come to your home to measure your kitchen and give you a price quotation; generally there is no charge for this.

As with stock and custom modular bids, make sure your plan is specific enough to obtain a reliable quote and to eliminate any misunderstanding as to what you're ordering.

Typical Cabinets

Stock and modular cabinets come in many styles—here is a representative variety

Just as appliances come in standard sizes, so do cabinets. Look around your kitchen; you'll see base cabinets that sit on the floor and wall cabinets that screw to the wall. All kitchens contain some combination of these two, and most include a few variations that don't quite fit in either category. Illustrated on these two pages are a few of the many different styles and configurations of stock and modular cabinets.

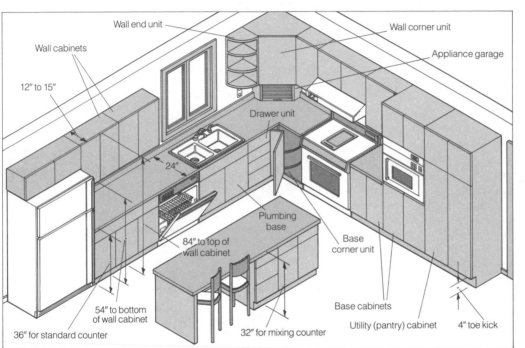

Wall end unit
Wall cabinets
12" to 15"
Wall corner unit
Appliance garage
Drawer unit
24"
84" to top of wall cabinet
Plumbing base
Base corner unit
54" to bottom of wall cabinet
36" for standard counter
32" for mixing counter
Base cabinets
Utility (pantry) cabinet
4" toe kick

Basic units of cabinetry

Typical kitchen utilizes base cabinets, upper wall cabinets, and upper and lower corner and end units. In addition, you can get 7- or 8-foot-tall utility cabinets, special bases that hold a kitchen sink, and matching facades for dishwasher, refrigerator, and other appliances.

Straight upper wall cabinets

Wall cabinets come in singles, doubles, and various specialty configurations. Typically 12 (or 15) inches deep, they can vary in width from 9 to 60 inches. Though the most frequently used heights are 15, 18, and 30 inches, wall cabinets range from 12 to 36 inches high, or more.

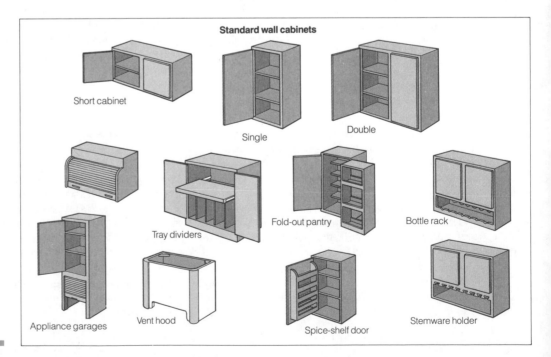

Standard wall cabinets

Short cabinet
Single
Double
Tray dividers
Fold-out pantry
Bottle rack
Appliance garages
Vent hood
Spice-shelf door
Stemware holder

Upper corners and ends

Special cabinets take advantage of areas where upper wall cabinets terminate or turn a corner. End cabinets offer simple shelves or narrow enclosures. Corner cabinets may have angled or curved doors, tamboured appliance garages, or lazy Susans. These cabinets are sized to match other wall cabinets.

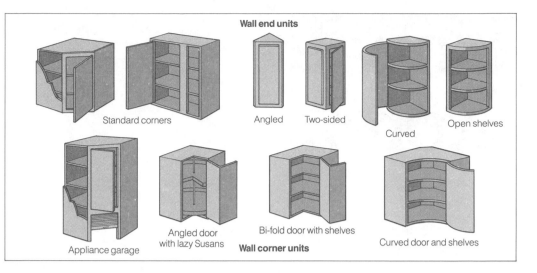

Wall end units

Standard corners

Angled Two-sided

Curved

Open shelves

Appliance garage

Angled door with lazy Susans

Wall corner units

Bi-fold door with shelves

Curved door and shelves

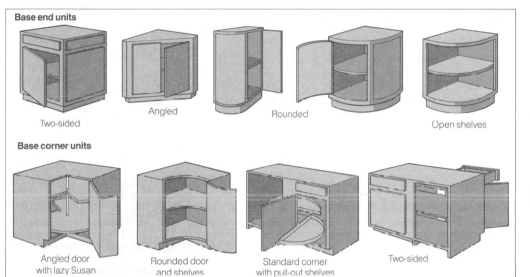

Base end units

Two-sided

Angled

Rounded

Open shelves

Base corner units

Angled door with lazy Susan

Rounded door and shelves

Standard corner with pull-out shelves

Two-sided

Base corners and ends

Corner base units come in at least a dozen configurations; a few are shown here. Lazy Susans and diagonal units use space efficiently. End cabinets may offer storage accessible from both front and side.

Base cabinets

When complete with a toe kick or plinth, base cabinets normally measure 34½ inches tall; the counter adds another 1½ inches. In width, they range from 9 to 60 inches, increasing in increments of 3 inches from 9 to 36 inches and increments of 6 inches after that. Standard depth is 24 inches. Typically, a base cabinet offers one shelf and a drawer above a door, but—as you can see— many options are available.

Base cabinets

Standard base cabinet

Drawer unit

Wire baskets

Drawers and cutting board

Vertical dividers

Pull-out shelves

Shallow cabinet

Fold-out pantry

How To Store...

What is the best way to store a food processor? How about large bowls or pans? What about onions? Every element that goes into the kitchen should be stored appropriately— but what is appropriate for the variety of utensils, foods, and other items we store?

This chapter focuses on the best ways to deal with the foods and paraphernalia we pack into our kitchens. Alphabetically, it offers an item-by-item catalog of both standard and creative answers to specific kitchen storage needs.

Appliances

Sometimes small appliance storage involves no more than pushing a blender into a corner. But with the proliferation of kitchen appliances, counters can be overrun in no time with toasters, coffee makers, can openers, juicers, blenders, and so on. Less-used appliances, such as waffle irons and slow-cookers, often disappear into the forgotten recesses of cabinetry. Shown on these two pages are a few better ways to store small appliances.

Convenient base-cabinet storage

Small appliances, particularly those needed infrequently, can be stored in corners of base cabinets— just be sure to provide easy access for handling their large, bulky shapes. Interior corner offers lazy Susan, end cabinet opens on two sides. Large, lower drawers can hold smallest appliances.

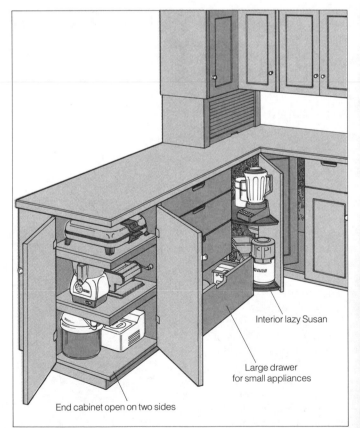

Interior lazy Susan

Large drawer for small appliances

End cabinet open on two sides

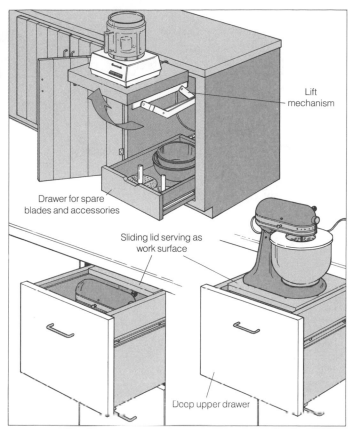

Lift mechanism

Drawer for spare blades and accessories

Sliding lid serving as work surface

Deep upper drawer

Pull-outs, swing-ups, and space savers

At left, lift mechanism brings heavy appliances up to counter height, adds to work surface; accessories store below it. Sliding lid on deep upper drawer serves as surface for mixer or appliance stored inside. Below, a number of kitchen appliances are available in space-saving versions. Cabinet- and wall-mounted styles mount easily; built-ins are a bit more challenging.

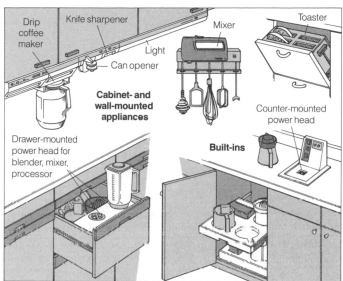

Drip coffee maker

Knife sharpener

Light

Can opener

Mixer

Toaster

Cabinet- and wall-mounted appliances

Counter-mounted power head

Drawer-mounted power head for blender, mixer, processor

Built-ins

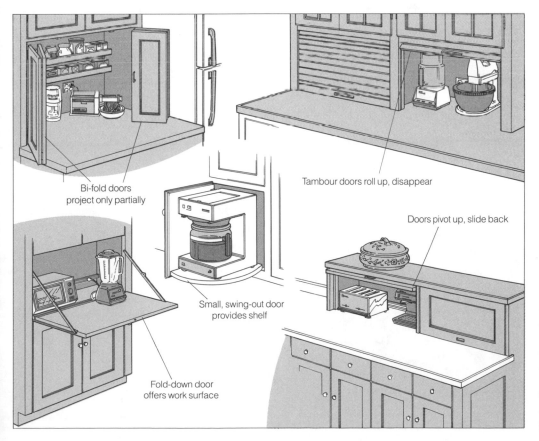

Bi-fold doors project only partially

Tambour doors roll up, disappear

Doors pivot up, slide back

Small, swing-out door provides shelf

Fold-down door offers work surface

Appliances behind doors

Doors that work best for enclosing small appliances are those that stay out of the way when they are open. Bi-folds, tambours, fold-downs, and pivoting/sliding doors are favorites. Stock hardware is available for all.

Bottles

What are the best ways to store soda, liquor, vinegar, oil, and other products that come in tall, awkwardly shaped, breakable bottles? On these two pages, you'll find helpful storage ideas for bottled products.

Wine requires a little extra consideration. To store it properly, place wine on its side and keep it at a relatively cool, constant temperature (around 60°F/16°C), away from bright sunlight and vibration. In an air-conditioned house, location is less critical than in a house with fluctuating temperatures. Don't worry about jug wines or other wines you intend to drink soon after purchase—just place them upright, anywhere that's cool.

Pull-out racks

For efficient storage of bottles and all sorts of other goods, cabinetmakers and manufacturers can install coated-wire pull-out racks in various configurations.

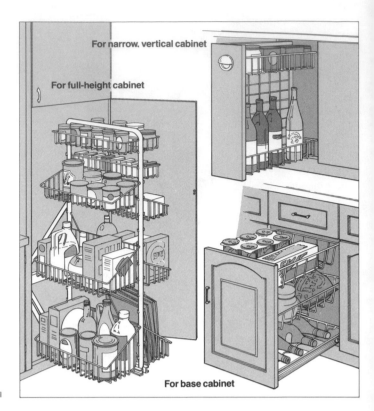

For narrow, vertical cabinet

For full-height cabinet

For base cabinet

Bottle drawers and shelves

Store bottles deep in your cabinets by placing them in drawers. Drawer inserts available through some cabinet shops keep bottles organized and upright. Shallow shelves also provide easy access to bottles. For horizontal wine storage, you can buy stock cubbyhole cabinets or add notched wooden strips to shelves.

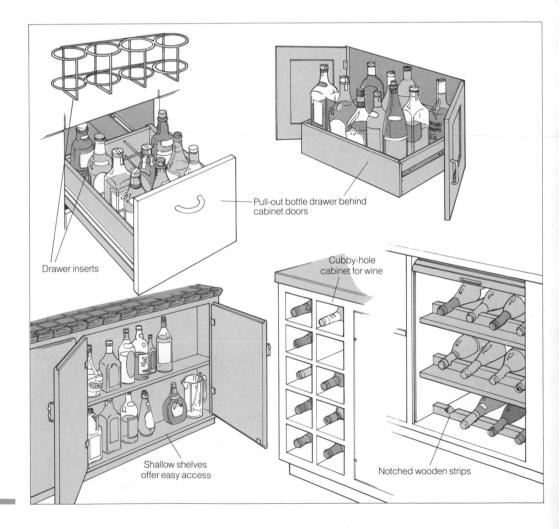

Drawer inserts

Pull-out bottle drawer behind cabinet doors

Shallow shelves offer easy access

Cubby-hole cabinet for wine

Notched wooden strips

Easy-to-make wine racks

Wine bottles stay organized and accessible in these three easy-to-make racks. At upper left, 6-inch lengths of 4-inch-diameter PVC pipe are glued together and installed in a base cabinet. At right, store-bought shelf tracks and brackets support 1 by 2s cut to hold wine bottles. Stacking, modular rack at lower left is made by cutting half-circles and interlocking ⅜-inch by ¾-inch notches in pine 1 by 4s.

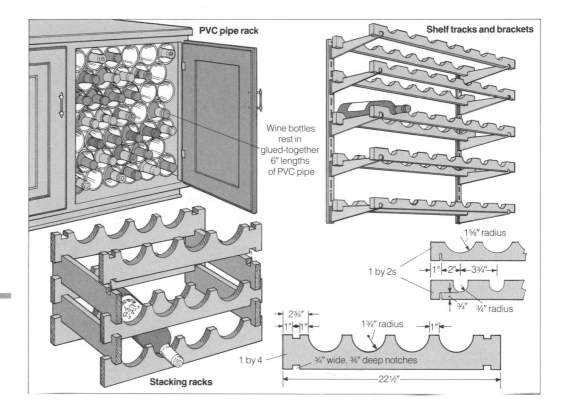

PVC pipe rack

Wine bottles rest in glued-together 6" lengths of PVC pipe

Shelf tracks and brackets

1⅝" radius

1 by 2s

1" 2" 3¾"

¾" ¾" radius

2¾"

1" 1"

1¾" radius

1"

1 by 4

¾" wide, ⅜" deep notches

22½"

Stacking racks

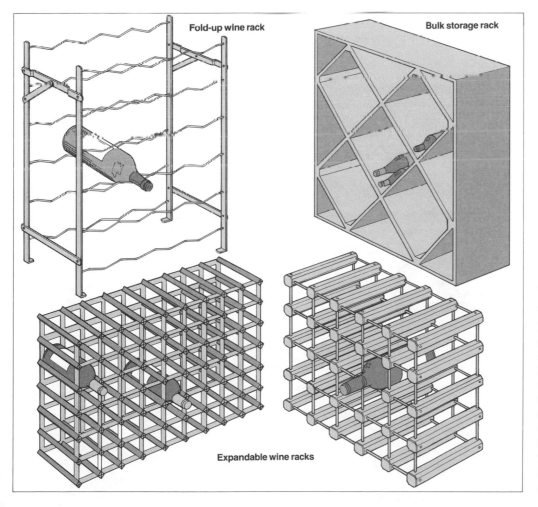

Fold-up wine rack

Bulk storage rack

Expandable wine racks

Wine racks you can buy

Many styles of wine racks are sold at specialty and department stores. Some, like fold-up version at upper left, hold a given number of bottles; others expand to grow with your collection. Model at upper right lets you stack bottles within cubicles for maximum use of space.

Cleaning Supplies

Is the cabinet under your kitchen sink a catchall for jumbled sponges, dishcloths, scouring pads, detergent, and cleanser? Are mops and brooms tangled together in a closet? Cleanup is rarely fun, but you can make it less of a chore through effective organization and accessible storage of supplies. Here are a few ideas for organizing your cleaning gear.

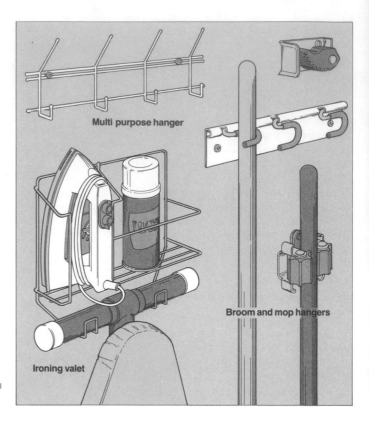

Cleanup hang-ups

Simple organizers make broom closets or utility cabinets tidy. Available at hardware stores and home-improvement centers, special hangers hold broom and mop handles, cleaning supplies— even ironing gear.

Multi purpose hanger

Broom and mop hangers

Ironing valet

Ultimate undersink cabinet

To maximize the awkward space beneath the kitchen sink, turn it into a cleanup center with pull-out trash can and wire storage bins and door-mounted racks for paper towels, grocery bags, dishtowels, and cleansers. Tilt-out tray in front of sink holds sponges and scrubbers. If you have small children in your home, don't forget to add childproof latches to cabinet doors.

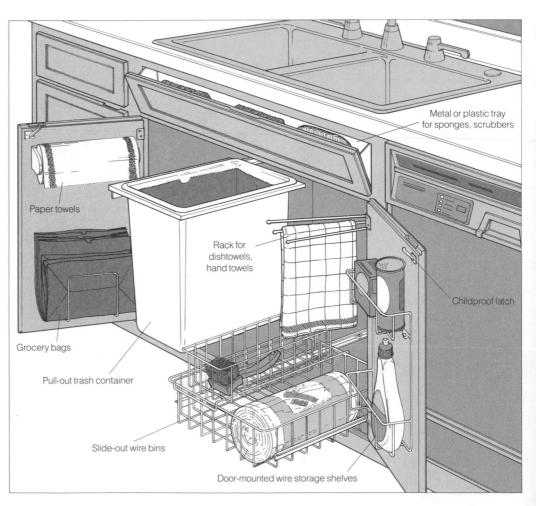

Paper towels

Grocery bags

Pull-out trash container

Slide-out wire bins

Metal or plastic tray for sponges, scrubbers

Rack for dishtowels, hand towels

Childproof latch

Door-mounted wire storage shelves

Holding the bags

Grocery bags stay put if slipped between vertical dividers in a narrow cabinet. Or you can build a simple rack into wall between studs or buy a wire holder to mount on a cabinet door.

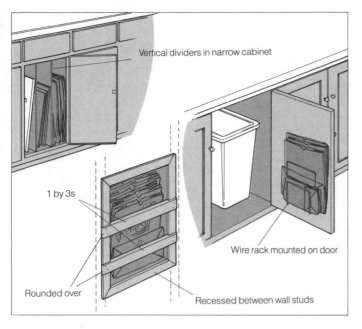

Vertical dividers in narrow cabinet

1 by 3s

Rounded over

Wire rack mounted on door

Recessed between wall studs

Cleanser carryalls

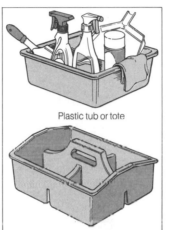

Plastic tub or tote

Household cleaning supplies can be stored under the sink in a small plastic tub or utility tote, then moved en masse to wherever they're needed on cleaning day.

Paper towel holders

Keep paper towels handy by mounting a holder to the underside of a cabinet or onto the backsplash wall, fitting one inside a cabinet (accessible by means of a slot cut in the bottom shelf), or setting out a freestanding model on the countertop.

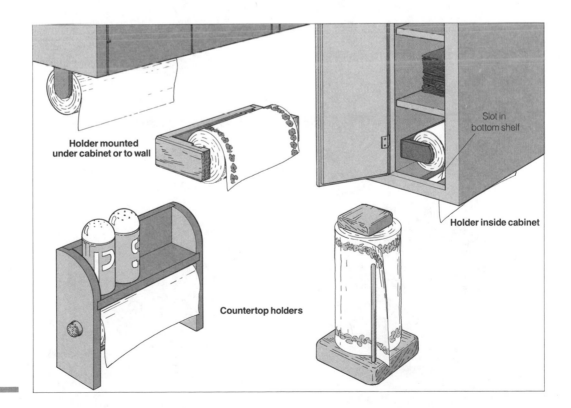

Holder mounted under cabinet or to wall

Slot in bottom shelf

Holder inside cabinet

Countertop holders

Cutlery & Flatware

When the vegetables are chopped and butter begins to melt in the pan, you don't want to have to go on a spatula hunt. If you seem to be burning butter frequently in pursuit of the right cooking implement, perhaps it's time to organize your utensils.

An efficient kitchen has drawers divided to keep flatware and cooking utensils tidy. Knives are stored safely, conveniently, and in a way that won't dull their edges. Many cabinet manufacturers now offer drawers with dividers as part of their stock cabinetry. In addition, you can buy any of a number of divided trays or baskets to slip into drawers.

Valuable silver should be stored in a secure place—perhaps a compartment behind a false kick-space panel. Wherever you put silver, enclose it in layers of flannel or special tarnish-retardant cloth to block air flow and cut down on the need for polishing.

Store-bought knife racks

A purchased knife rack can be mounted on the wall or on the inside surface of a cabinet door, or a knife block can sit on top of the counter near your preparation area. Look for these and similar models at department, cookware, and cutlery stores.

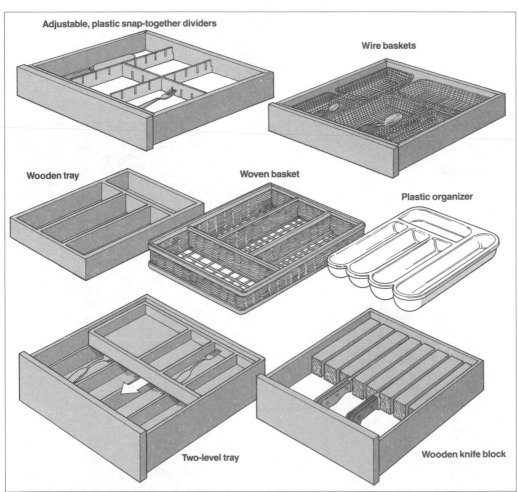

Drawer organizers for flatware and knives

Compartmented organizers keep flatware, knives, and other utensils sorted and help minimize scratches and dulled blades. You can choose from a wide variety of such dividers, from woven baskets to custom two-level trays.

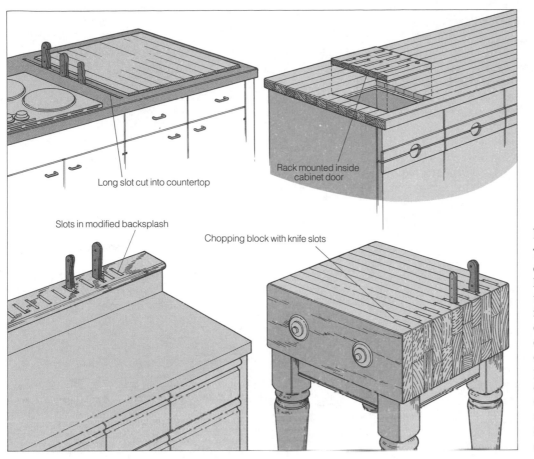

Long slot cut into countertop

Rack mounted inside cabinet door

Slots in modified backsplash

Chopping block with knife slots

Drop-in knives

To minimize countertop clutter and still keep knives where you need them, build a knife block into the counter. Or you can use specially made chopping blocks or modifications to countertops to provide convenient storage. Just be sure blades extend down into unused space, so they can't cut anyone.

Knife holders you can make

Here are two knife racks you can make yourself— a freestanding wooden knife block and an acrylic-covered wall rack.

For the block, use a radial arm or table saw to cut grooves down the entire length of a 4-foot 2 by 8, making them half the desired finished depth. Cut the board into four equal lengths and, with grooves aligned, glue, clamp, sand, and apply oil or other clear finish.

Wall rack is easy to assemble from 1 by 2s and a 1/8- or 1/4-inch clear acrylic sheet.

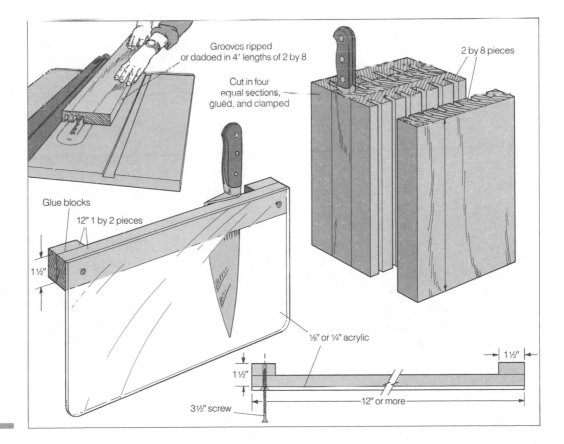

Grooves ripped or dadoed in 4′ lengths of 2 by 8

2 by 8 pieces

Cut in four equal sections, glued, and clamped

Glue blocks

12″ 1 by 2 pieces

1½″

1/8″ or 1/4″ acrylic

1½″

3½″ screw

1½″

12″ or more

Dishes & Glassware

Store everyday dishes and glassware in cabinets that are convenient to the dishwasher, refrigerator, and serving areas. Shelves in upper cabinets are usually most convenient. Some people prefer base-cabinet drawers for dishes—but remember that they can chip or crack if drawers are slammed or moved too abruptly.

It's often best to store tableware used mostly for entertaining near the dining room. You may want to display china, crystal, and silver behind glass doors. If so, consider glass shelves for unobstructed viewing.

Custom shelving to organize dinnerware

The more fitted shelving is to its contents, the more efficiently it utilizes space. Here are examples of custom shelving that both organizes and displays its contents.

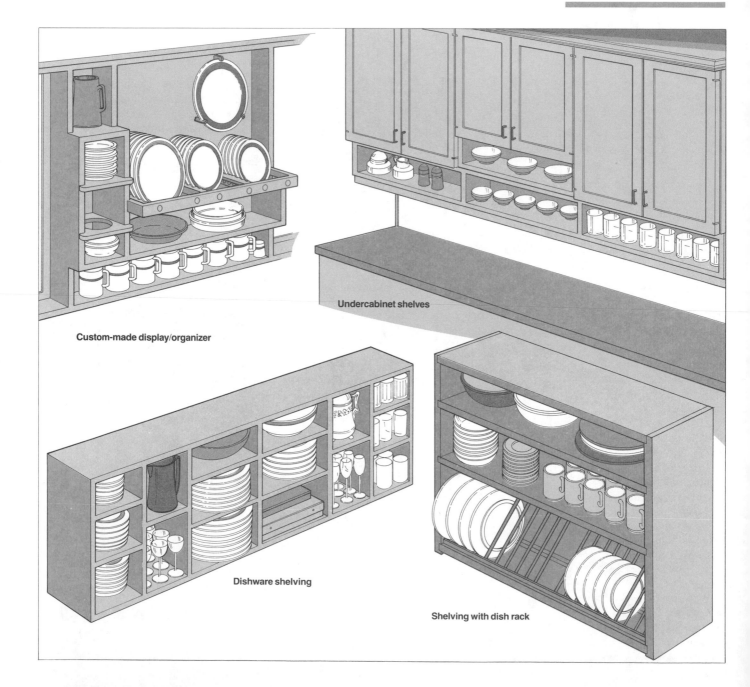

Custom-made display/organizer

Undercabinet shelves

Dishware shelving

Shelving with dish rack

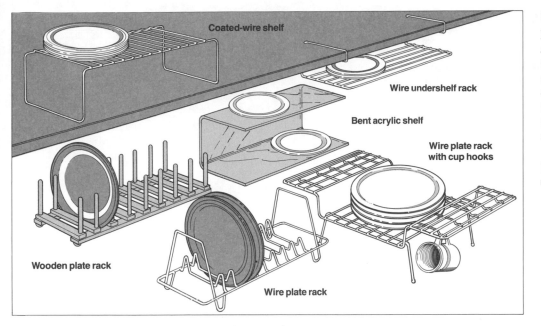

Coated-wire shelf

Wire undershelf rack

Bent acrylic shelf

Wire plate rack
with cup hooks

Wooden plate rack

Wire plate rack

Shelf maximizers

Numerous products are available for extending the storage capacity of standard shelves. These organizers can double or triple usable space, protect dishes, and make access easier.

For more examples, see pages 42 and 43.

Stemware hangers

Inexpensive and effective commercially available hangers for stemware can be mounted to the underside of upper cabinets, onto cabinet sides, or directly to walls. (Also see page 43.)

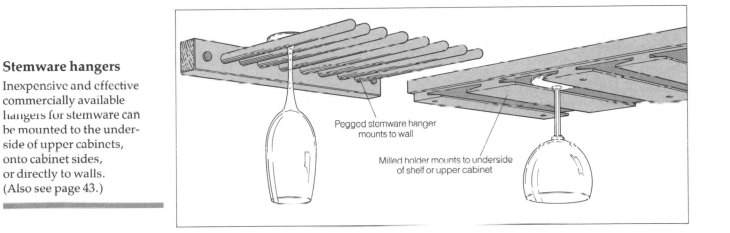

Pegged stemware hanger mounts to wall

Milled holder mounts to underside of shelf or upper cabinet

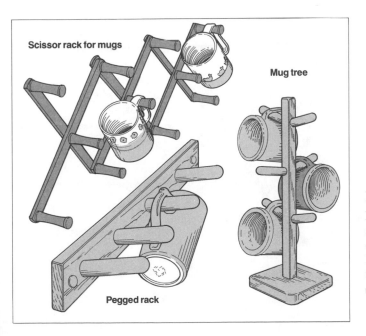

Scissor rack for mugs

Mug tree

Pegged rack

Mug racks

Mugs can take up considerable cabinet space. Instead of setting them on shelves, hang mugs from inexpensive wall- or door-mounted racks. You can buy a "scissor" rack that holds many mugs, a Shaker-style peg rack, or a freestanding mug tree.

Foods: Boxed & Canned

The average American kitchen is stocked with more canned and boxed foods than any other type of edibles: canned soups, vegetables, fruits, meats; boxed cereals, crackers, pastry mixes; and many more packaged foods. Not only are these products easy to serve—they're easy to store and long-lived if unopened. Canned meat, fish, vegetables, and soups last up to 2 years in dry, relatively cool cupboards. Unopened cereals and boxed goods typically last from 3 to 12 months in cool, dry, vermin-free storage. On these two pages, you'll find a number of ways to get the most from your cupboards when storing boxed and canned foods.

Shelves and drawers for boxes and cans

Shelves, drawers, and drawer-like baskets are common facilities for storing boxes and cans. Upper-cabinet shelves, typically 12 inches deep, allow easy access to a single line-up of boxes.

By slanting deep shelves and adding a lip to the front edge (upper right), you can create deep storage that automatically feeds cans toward the front when you pull one out—a method that works well if you store multiples of certain foods or drinks.

For deeper lower cabinets, pull-outs work best. Baskets or drawers with short fronts allow you to locate goods before pulling them out.

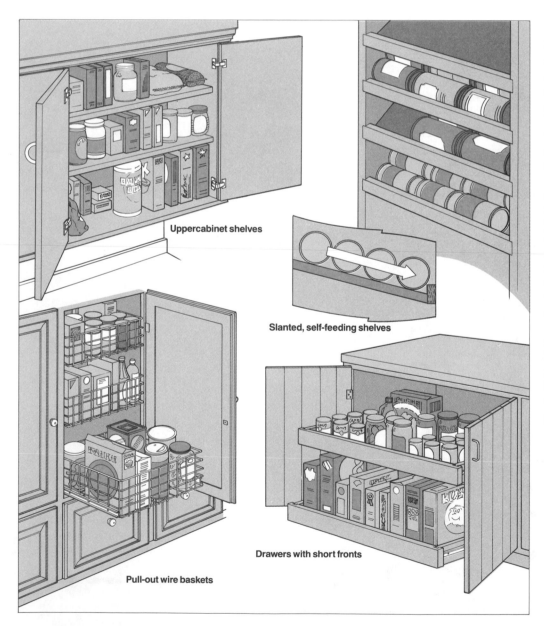

Uppercabinet shelves

Slanted, self-feeding shelves

Pull-out wire baskets

Drawers with short fronts

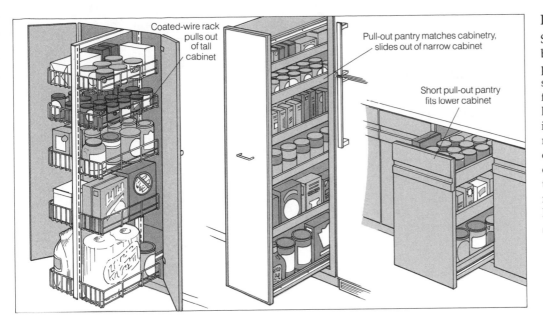

Coated-wire rack pulls out of tall cabinet

Pull-out pantry matches cabinetry, slides out of narrow cabinet

Short pull-out pantry fits lower cabinet

Pull-out pantries

Sliding smoothly on ball-bearing glides, pull-out pantries offer efficient storage for cans and boxed foods. Coated-wire rack has adjustable shelves, fits in tall, narrow space. Narrow wooden rack matches cabinets. Short rack in deep cabinet uses space that would be hard to reach without pull-out hardware.

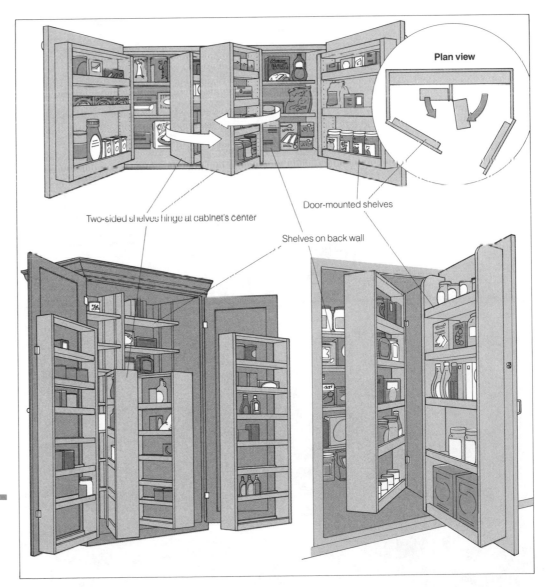

Plan view

Door-mounted shelves

Two-sided shelves hinge at cabinet's center

Shelves on back wall

Fold-out food storage

Loaded with storage for boxes, cans, and jars, fold-out pantries have several layers of shelving—mounted on the back wall, attached to the door, and pivoting on hinges at cabinet's center. Such systems are relatively expensive but worth the money if storage space is tight.

Foods: Dry Goods

Rice, flour, pasta, cereals, and other similar foods will keep for a long time if properly stored. Most dry goods last about a year (the rising agent in self-rising flour may degenerate after about 6 months). But because of the threat of insects spreading among grains and other dry goods, the best storage is in sealed containers where the foods remain isolated and dry. Keep foods near where you will use them.

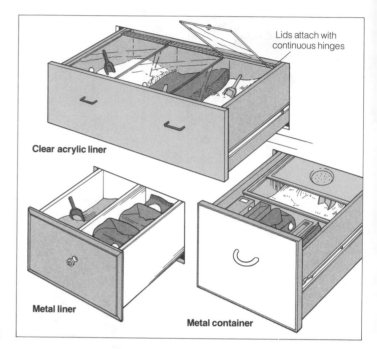

Lids attach with continuous hinges

Clear acrylic liner

Metal liner

Metal container

Drawers for dry goods

Metal or plastic liners in drawers can provide convenient, sealed storage for dry goods. Some types of drawer liners are available as stock items. Others, such as the clear acrylic liner shown at top, must be custom fabricated.

Storage containers

Airtight cannisters, clear plastic stackable containers, jars with tight-fitting lids—you'll find a wide variety of storage containers made for storing pastas, beans, nuts, and other dry goods. The classic bread box keeps breads dry and close at hand.

Foods: Produce

The refrigerator is a kitchen's main facility for storing produce, but not the only one. Fruit baskets, coated-wire baskets, and even old-fashioned cooling cupboards vented to the outdoors are a few other possibilities. Different fruits and vegetables may require different storage conditions—listed below are a few guidelines.

■ Though chilled storage isn't mandatory for fruits and vegetables, most produce lasts longer in the refrigerator. Refrigerate most fruits and vegetables unwashed (so they remain dry), in plastic or paper bags. Though most vegetables stay freshest in plastic bags, some (corn, chives, mushrooms, whole squash, and lettuce, for example) keep best wrapped in paper towels first. Be sure to seal cut melons in plastic bags—they give off ethylene gas, which can hasten spoilage of other produce in the refrigerator.

■ Garlic, dry onions, and potatoes keep best unwrapped in a cool (50° F), dry, dark place with good ventilation (they'll last up to 2 months).

■ Unripe fruit such as avocados or pears ripens best when placed in a loosely closed paper bag at room temperature (turn fruit occasionally). Leave bananas uncovered at room temperature to ripen.

■ Tomatoes can be stored unwashed at room temperature, stem end down, until slightly soft, then refrigerated.

■ Avoid storing overly ripe, bruised, or damaged produce. The bad apple *will* spoil the whole bunch.

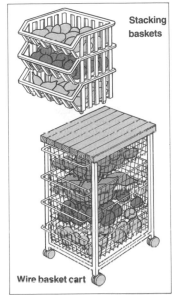

Wire basket cart

Stacking or rolling baskets

Coated-wire or plastic baskets offer ventilated storage for fruits and vegetables that don't require refrigeration—especially those you'll be eating within a couple of days. Storing in cool, dark areas is best.

Drawers and bins

Cabinetmakers can build custom drawers or bins for produce. Tilt-down glass or plastic-front bins are a popular choice for fruits that don't require air circulation, such as citrus. Mesh-bottom or front ventilated drawers or basket inserts can store garlic, dry onions, and potatoes.

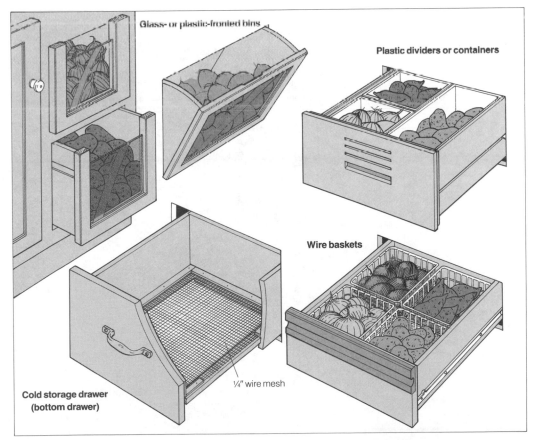

Glass- or plastic-fronted bins

Plastic dividers or containers

Wire baskets

Cold storage drawer (bottom drawer)

¼" wire mesh

Linens for Dining

The ideal storage for table linens keeps them wrinkle-free. With placemats and napkins, this is relatively easy; large tablecloths present more of a challenge. Placemats and napkins can be kept neat in shallow drawers or on short shelves. Tablecloths store best when hung from dowels or slats. If your cabinets can't provide the generous space needed for hanging table-cloths, you can minimize wrinkles by rolling the cloths around large mailing tubes and giving the rolls plenty of room in a shallow drawer.

Racks for tablecloths

If your cabinets are roomy enough, a wall-mounted or pull-out rack is the best way to store tablecloths. Such racks are easy to make from standard lumber and dowels; pull-out rack mounts on standard drawer glides.

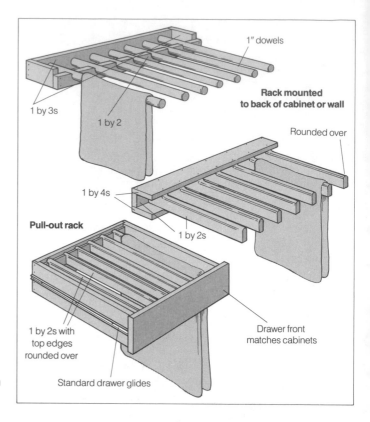

1" dowels

Rack mounted to back of cabinet or wall

1 by 3s

1 by 2

Rounded over

1 by 4s

Pull-out rack

1 by 2s

1 by 2s with top edges rounded over

Standard drawer glides

Drawer front matches cabinets

Napkin and placemat placement

Shallow drawers provide convenient, dust-free storage for placemats and napkins. Closely spaced shelves, pull-out baskets, and wire trays that hang from shelves are other good solutions.

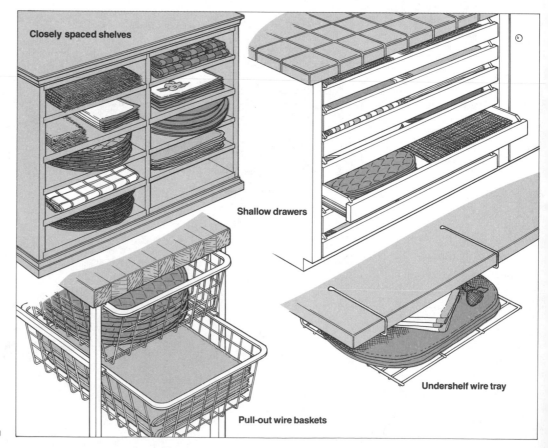

Closely spaced shelves

Shallow drawers

Pull-out wire baskets

Undershelf wire tray

Mixing Bowls

Though large bowls are indispensible for preparing and serving food, they top the list of space-gobblers in cabinets. When designing your kitchen storage system, it's important to provide ample, appropriate storage for large bowls.

Where you put them will depend upon how frequently they're needed. Some you may use daily, while others—a large punch bowl, for example—can stay stashed away for occasional parties. Bowls you use often can be stored in base cabinets on pull-out drawers or corner carousels where they're easy to get to but don't block other supplies. Find space for infrequently needed bowls on top shelves of upper cabinets, or even in another room.

Shallow drawers

Pull-out wire baskets

Lazy-Susan corner carousel

Bowls in base cabinets

Large bowls stay accessible yet out of the way if you place them in shallow drawers behind cabinet doors, in pull-out baskets, or on lazy-Susan carousels in corner cabinets. Base cabinets generally accommodate big bowls best; heavy-duty hardware may be neccessary for drawer glides.

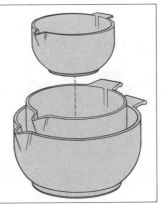

Bowls that nest

When buying bowls, opt for the kind that nest. A set of several won't take up any more space than a single bowl.

Pots & Pans

Whether you need a family-size stockpot for simmering soup or a tiny pan for melting butter, you'll want to have your pots and pans within easy reach of cooktop and oven. Because they are so bulky, pots and pans are often stored in base cabinets. But putting them on standard shelves usually results in a jumbled pile. Use heavy-duty drawers and pull-out trays behind doors for more convenient storage of cookware.

Pots and pans also can be treated as a decorative element. As shown on the facing page, a variety of racks is available for hanging pots and pans from walls or ceilings, keeping them out of the cupboard altogether. One note about racks: because of the weight they will bear, you must be careful to hang them according to manufacturer's directions.

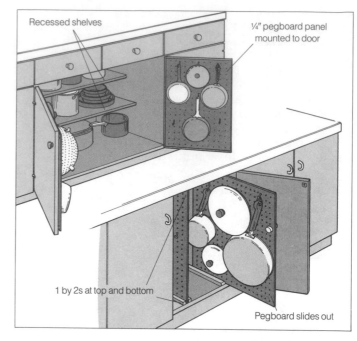

Recessed shelves

¼" pegboard panel mounted to door

1 by 2s at top and bottom

Pegboard slides out

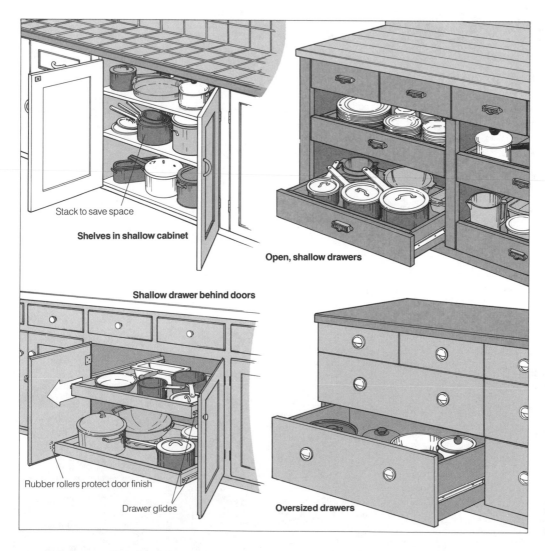

Stack to save space

Shelves in shallow cabinet

Open, shallow drawers

Shallow drawer behind doors

Rubber rollers protect door finish

Drawer glides

Oversized drawers

Pegboard pull-outs

Make your own hangers for pots, pans, and lids inside cabinets by using ¼-inch pegboard panels. Use wooden spacers to attach pegboard to cabinet doors in order to give clearance for hooks. For slide-out racks, cut each panel slightly smaller than height and depth of cabinet so it moves freely between pairs of 1 by 2s screwed to top and bottom of cabinet interior.

Shelves and drawers for pots and pans

Pots and pans can be difficult to retrieve from deep shelves in standard base cabinets. Choose shallow cabinets for easier access, or put pots and pans in pull-out shelves or drawers on heavy-duty glides. Small rubber rollers attached to drawer corners protect doors from damage when drawers are pulled open.

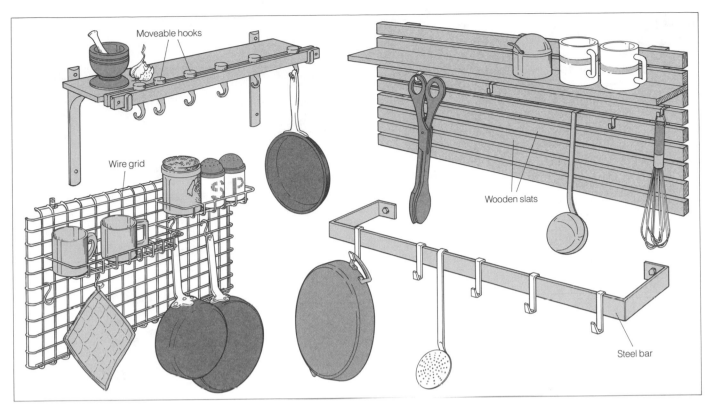

Moveable hooks

Wire grid

Wooden slats

Steel bar

Wall-mounted pan racks

For both decorative and functional storage, you can buy any of a number of pan racks and grids that mount to the wall. Follow manufacturers instructions for installation; often racks must be fastened to wall studs because of the weight they will bear.

Hanging pan racks

Suspended from ceiling hooks, hanging pan racks can create a dramatic focal point in the kitchen. Best placement is generally above a counter near the cooktop or over a nearby island unit where pots and pans won't be in the way of traffic.

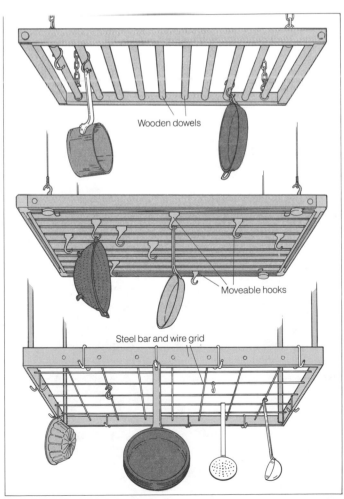

Wooden dowels

Moveable hooks

Steel bar and wire grid

Spices

Almost every kitchen has a healthy collection of jars, tins, shakers, and boxes of spices and herbs. Arranging them is a challenge. There's a wide range of sizes and shapes to contend with, yet many containers look exactly alike except for the name on the label. How can you store seasonings so they're close to where you use them—usually the cooktop or food preparation center—and easy to distinguish from one another?

Here's an illustrated assortment of spice racks to solve the problem, many making use of often-overlooked kitchen space. Whichever arrangement you choose, display spices so they can be recognized at a glance; you don't want to sprinkle cayenne pepper into a dish calling for cinnamon.

Generally, spice and herb containers should be stored away from direct heat, moisture, and light. Keep the tops tightly closed between use to prevent loss of flavor.

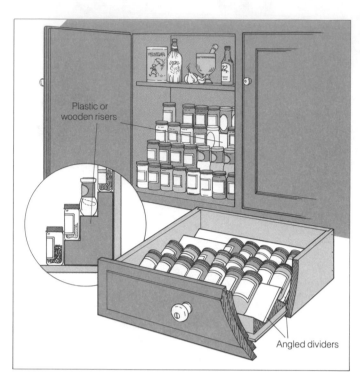

Angled and stepped organizers

Angled dividers tip spices into view and allow bottles to fit in shallow drawers. Stepped organizer at top lines spice bottles up in several tiers on cabinet shelf, keeping each row in view. These kinds of organizers can be purchased premade, or you can make your own from scrap wood.

Swing-out spices

Upper cabinets near the cooktop are convenient places to store spices. Two possibilities are shown here. Coated-wire racks at left hold spices on inside of cabinet door. Hinged, double-sided spice rack, right, holds twice the spice. Both types require recessing interior cabinet shelves to give clearance.

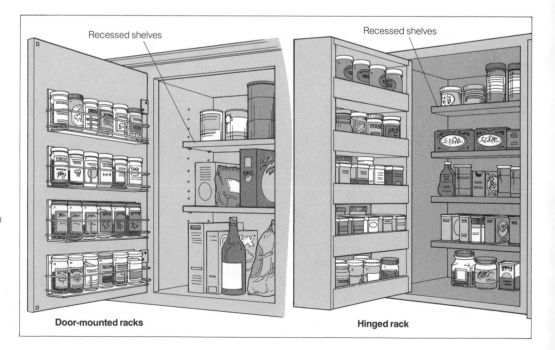

Door-mounted racks

Hinged rack

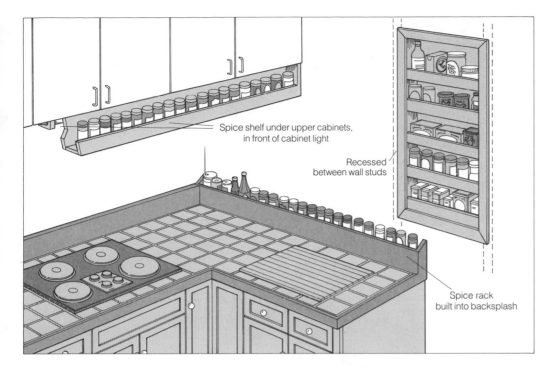

Spice shelf under upper cabinets, in front of cabinet light

Recessed between wall studs

Spice rack built into backsplash

Built-in spice racks

Consider built-in spice racks when remodeling or installing new cabinets. Add a spice shelf beneath upper cabinets, provide a rack along the backsplash, or recess shelves between wall studs.

Pull-out spice storage

In narrow upper or lower cabinet, you can install a tall, two-sided spice cupboard that pulls out on standard full-extension drawer glides.

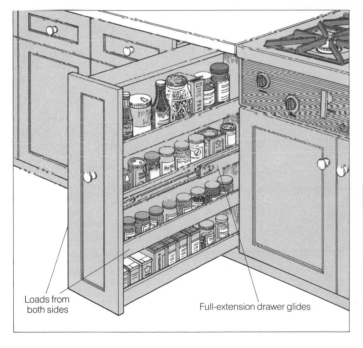

Loads from both sides

Full-extension drawer glides

Freestanding spice racks

Cookware, specialty, and department stores sell many types of freestanding racks and turntables to keep spices organized and convenient. Some include bottles—for a uniform look—and labels that help the busy cook locate a particular spice quickly.

Trash & Items to Recycle

Efficient and orderly ways of dealing with kitchen wastes can put an end to messy, overflowing waste-baskets, unpleasant odors, and some of the drudgery of garbage and recycling duty.

Once you locate all the waste production points in your kitchen—such as the can opener, food prepara-tion counter, and chopping block—you may find that the best place for the kitchen garbage receptacle is under or near the kitchen sink. Always line the waste-basket with a heavy-duty grocery bag or plastic liner; your wastebasket will stay cleaner, and your trash will be more likely to make it outside to the garbage can in one uneventful trip. For the ultimate in trash space-saving, you can install a trash compactor that can compress what would fill three to four 20-gallon gar-bage cans into one odorless, leakproof, disposable bag.

If you're a gardener, you may want to keep organic wastes in a separate container to add to a compost pile. And if you have room in your kitchen, you can put recyclables in separate receptacles to save sorting time later on. Aluminum and tin cans (flattened), glass bottles and jars, newspapers, and paper bags are all recyclable.

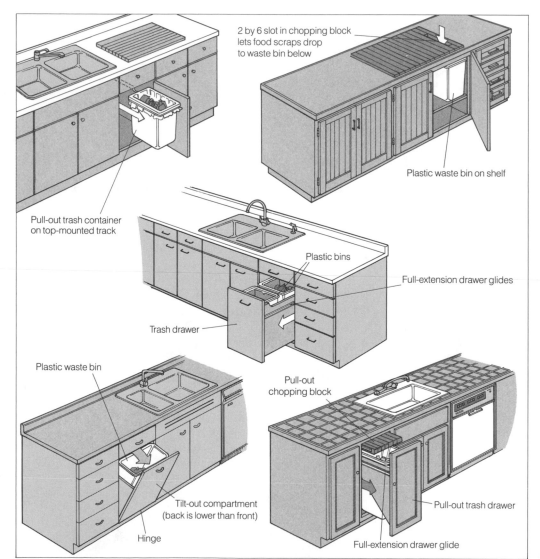

2 by 6 slot in chopping block lets food scraps drop to waste bin below

Plastic waste bin on shelf

Pull-out trash container on top-mounted track

Plastic bins

Full-extension drawer glides

Trash drawer

Plastic waste bin

Pull-out chopping block

Tilt-out compartment (back is lower than front)

Hinge

Pull-out trash drawer

Full-extension drawer glide

Built-in waste receptacles

When planning cabinets, it's easy to give trash and recyclables a place of their own. Cabinet manufactur-ers make pull-out trash containers, deep trash drawers, and tilt-out com-partments. Custom cabi-netmakers can duplicate these and offer other solutions as well, such as a slotted chopping block (upper right) to let food scraps drop to a waste bin below.

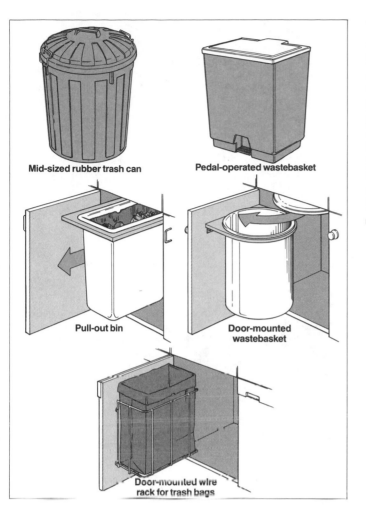

Mid-sized rubber trash can

Pedal-operated wastebasket

Pull-out bin

Door-mounted wastebasket

Door-mounted wire rack for trash bags

Trash containers

Choose a hard-working trash can for your kitchen. A mid-sized rubber one with a lid holds a generous amount of trash; this or a pedal-operated wastebasket can be left out in the kitchen. Containers that pull out or swing out on cabinet's door offer convenience—and stay hidden when not in use.

Recycling solutions

For the serious recycler, a recycling center provides space for newspapers, string, trash bags, tools, and plastic bins for bottles and cans. To crush cans easily, build a smasher from two lengths of 2 by 4 hinged together. Stack newspapers in a store-bought wire rack or a plywood box you make yourself.

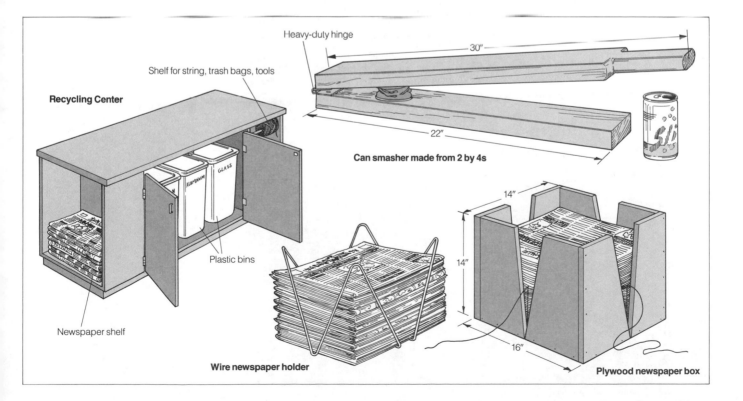

Recycling Center

Shelf for string, trash bags, tools

Heavy-duty hinge

30"

22"

Can smasher made from 2 by 4s

Plastic bins

Newspaper shelf

ALUMINUM GLASS

Wire newspaper holder

14"

14"

16"

Plywood newspaper box

Trays & Serving Equipment

Large cooky sheets, muffin tins, serving trays, baking pans, and similar kitchen equipment demand specialized storage. Most aren't needed on a daily basis, so they can be stored in out-of-the-way cabinets. But because of their large sizes and sometimes unusual shapes, they can consume copious amounts of space if not stored properly.

Deep cabinets above oven or refrigerator or narrow base cabinets are favored for tray storage. Dividers allow tidy, vertical storage so that any tray can be slipped out without disturbing the others.

Vertical cabinet dividers

Several methods can be used to create vertical cabinet dividers. These custom models include dowels inserted into holes in shelves above and below; manufactured wire dividers fitted into holes; short dividers in slotted base; and solid panel dividers.

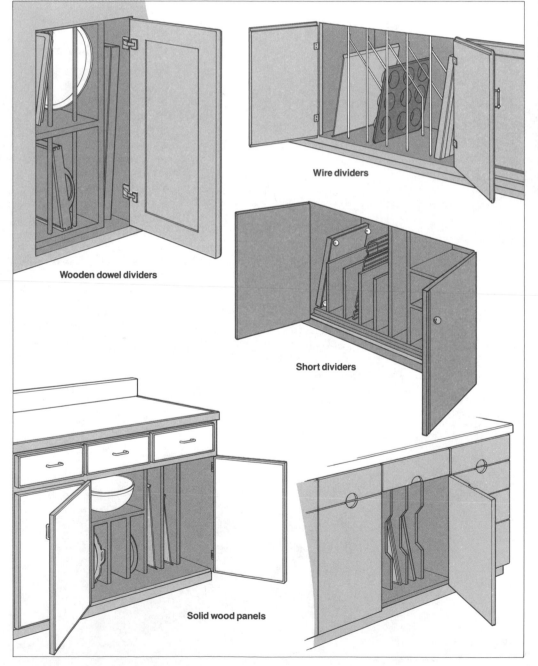

Wooden dowel dividers

Wire dividers

Short dividers

Solid wood panels

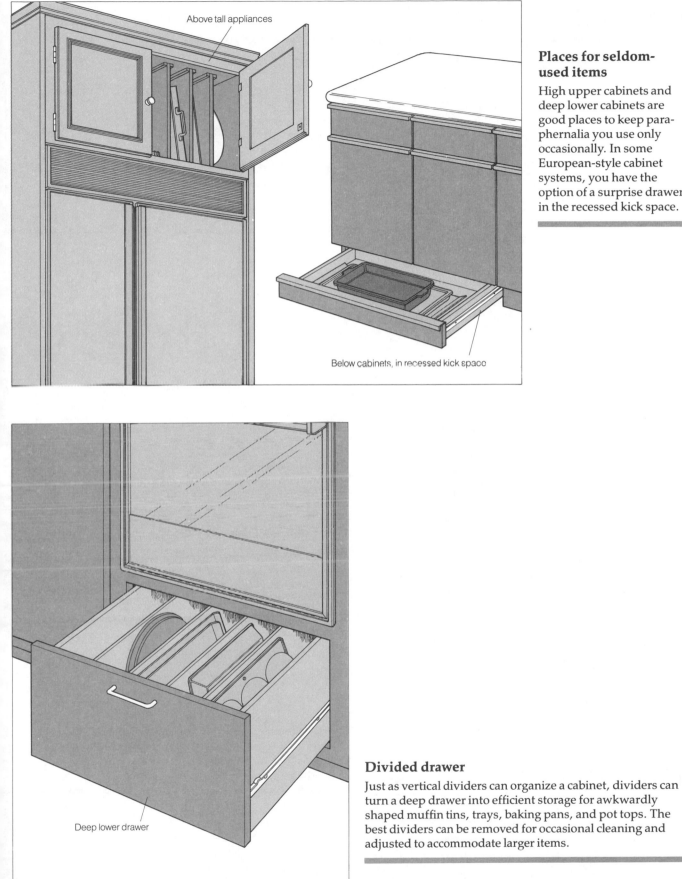

Above tall appliances

Below cabinets, in recessed kick space

Deep lower drawer

Places for seldom-used items

High upper cabinets and deep lower cabinets are good places to keep paraphernalia you use only occasionally. In some European-style cabinet systems, you have the option of a surprise drawer in the recessed kick space.

Divided drawer

Just as vertical dividers can organize a cabinet, dividers can turn a deep drawer into efficient storage for awkwardly shaped muffin tins, trays, baking pans, and pot tops. The best dividers can be removed for occasional cleaning and adjusted to accommodate larger items.

Sources

Manufacturers of kitchen cabinets and storage products

When you're transforming an old kitchen into one that's innovative and workable, you'll find a wealth of ideas and information in brochures put out by the various manufacturers of kitchen storage units. Here's a selection of major cabinet and storage product manufacturers who will send you information on request; they can also tell you about local outlets or distributors for their products.

The entries are coded to identify what each company manufactures; importers of European cabinetry are indicated as well. The product codes and addresses in this list are accurate as of press time.

The yellow pages of your telephone directory and the National Kitchen & Bath Association (124 Main Street, Hackettstown, NJ 07840) can help you locate kitchen showrooms, cabinetmakers, designers, architects, and other sources near you.

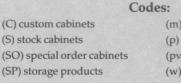

Codes:

(C) custom cabinets	(m) metal
(S) stock cabinets	(p) plastic
(SO) special order cabinets	(pv) plastic laminate veneer
(SP) storage products	(w) wood
	(i) imported

Adelphi
P.O. Box 10
Robesonia, PA 19551
(C, SO/w)

Akro-Mils, Inc.
P.O. Box 989
Akron, OH 44309
(SP/m, p)

Allmilmo Corporation
70 Clinton Rd.
Fairfield, NJ 07006
(SO/pv, w, i)

American Cabinet Concepts, Inc.
1021 Columbia Blvd.
Longview, WA 98632
(S, SO/pv, w)

Ampco
P.O. Box 608
Rosedale, MS 38769
(C/m)

Aristokraft Cabinets
P.O. Box 420
Jasper, IN 47546
(S/pv, w)

Art Wire
230 Fifth Ave.
New York, NY 10001
(SP/m)

Bertch Wood Specialties
4747 Crestwood Dr.
Waterloo, IA 50702
(C, SO/pv, w)

Birchcraft Kitchens, Inc.
1612 Thorn St.
Reading, PA 19601
(C/pv, w)

Bosch Corporation
2800 S. 25th Ave.
Broadview, IL 60153
(S/pv, w)

Capri Custom Cabinetry, Inc.
59 Armstrong Rd.
Plymouth, MA 02360
(C, S, SO/pv, w)

City Cabinetmakers
1351 Underwood Ave.
San Francisco, CA 94124
(C/pv, w)

Closet Maid, Clairson Int'l
720 SW 17th St.
Ocala, FL 32674
(SP/p)

Compagnucci USA, Inc.
14 E. 60th St.
New York, NY 10022
(SP/m)

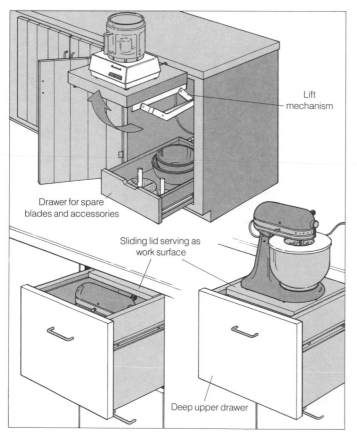

Lift mechanism

Drawer for spare blades and accessories

Sliding lid serving as work surface

Deep upper drawer

Cabinet manufacturers offer specialized fittings for all sorts of kitchen storage needs. Among available options are swing-up shelf for food processor or other appliance (top) and sliding drawer cover to serve as appliance work surface.

Coppes Napanee Kitchens
401 E. Market St.
Nappanee, IN 46550
(C/w)

Cottonwood
12757 S. State Street
Draper, UT 84020
(C, SO/pv, w)

Craft-Maid Custom Kitchens, Inc.
P.O. Box 4026
Reading, PA 19606
(C/pv, w)

Custom Wood Products, Inc.
P.O. Box 4516
Roanoke, VA 24015
(C/pv, w)

Diamond Cabinets
P.O. Box 547
Hillsboro, OR 97123
(S/w)

Elfa/Eurica Marketing, Inc.
14551 Franklin Ave. NW
Tustin, CA 92680
(SP/m, i)

Excel Wood Products Co., Inc.
One Excel Plaza
Lakewood, NJ 08701
(S/w)

Fieldstone Cabinetry, Inc.
P.O. Box 109
Northwood, IA 50459
(S, SO/w)

Grayline Housewares
1616 Berkeley St.
Elgin, IL 60123
(SP/m)

Grovener Industries
938B Clivedon Ave.
Annacis Business Park
Delta, B.C.
Canada V3M-5R5
(C, SO/pv, i)

Haas Cabinet Co., Inc.
625 W. Utica St.
Sellersburg, IN 47172
(S, SO/pv, w)

Hanssem Corp.
68 Veronica Ave.
Somerset, NJ 08873
(S, SO/pv)

Home Crest Corp.
P.O. Box 595
Goshen, IN 46526
(C, S/w)

Imperia Cabinet Corp.
1000 Main St.
Hanson, MA 02341
(C, SO/pv, w)

Imperial Cabinet Co., Inc.
P.O. Box 427
Gaston, IN 47342
(SO/w)

Iron-A-Way, Inc.
220 W. Jackson
Morton, IL 61550
(SP/m)

J Wood
P.O. Box 367
Milroy, PA 17063
(C/pv, w)

Kapri Kitchens
P.O. Box 100
Dallastown, PA 17313
(C/w)

Kemper Division
WCI, Inc.
701 S. N St.
Richmond, IN 47374
(S/pv, w)

Kent Moore Cabinets, Inc.
P.O. Box 3206
College Station, TX 77840
(C, SO/w)

Kitchen Kompact, Inc.
P.O. Box 868
Jeffersonville, IN 47130
(S/w)

Kraftmaid
16052 Industrial Parkway
Middlefield, OH 44062
(C, S, SO/pv, w)

Lager Kitchens
35 Agnes St.
East Providence, RI 02914
(C, S, SO/w)

LesCare Kitchens, Inc.
P.O. Box 3008
Waterbury, CT 06705
(C, SO/pv, w)

Merillat Industries, Inc.
5353 W. US 223
Adrian, MI 49221
(S/w)

Merit Kitchens
12185 86th Ave.
Surrey, B.C.
Canada V3W-3H8
(S/pv, w)

Millbrook
Route 20
Nassau, NY 12123
(S, C, SO/pv, w)

Northwood Products, Inc.
P.O. Box 2008
Coeur d'Alene, ID 83814
(C, S, SO/pv, w)

Pennville Custom Cabinetry
P.O. Box 1266
Portland, IN 47371
(C/w)

Perfection Wood Products
7645 York St.
Denver, CO 80229
(C, SO/pv, w)

Poggenpohl USA Corp.
6 Pearl Court
Allendale, NJ 07401
(C/pv, w, i)

Prestige Cabinet Corp. of America
29 Rider Place
Freeport, NY 11520
(C/pv)

Prestige Products, Inc.
P.O. Box 314
Neodesha, KS 66757
(S/w)

Quaker Maid Division
WCI, Inc.
Route 61
Leesport, PA 19533
(C, S/pv, w)

Ranier Woodworking Co.
16318 S. Meridian
Puyallup, WA 98373
(C/pv, w)

The Refacers, Inc.
1115 Landini Lane
Concord, CA 94520
(C, S, SO, SP, pv, w)

Renee Products
8600 Harrison Rd.
Cleves, OH 45002
(C, S/pv, w)

Rev-A-Shelf, Inc.
2409 Plantside Dr.
Jefferson, KY 40299
(SP/p)

Rubbermaid Inc.
1147 Akron Rd.
Wooster, OH 44691
(SP/p)

Rutt Custom Kitchens
Route 23
Goodville, PA 17528
(C/w)

Ryan Manufacturing Co.
Hager Cabinets
Box 1117
Mankato, MN 56001
(C/w)

Saint Charles Holdings, Inc.
1611 E. Main St.
Saint Charles, IL 60174
(C/pv, w)

Sawyer Cabinet, Inc.
12744 San Fernando Rd.
Sylmar, CA 91342
(C, S, SO/m, pv, w)

H.J. Scheirich Co.
P.O. Box 37120
Louisville, KY 40233
(S/w)

Starmark
P.O. Box 84810
Sioux Falls, SD 57118
(S/pv)

Style-Line Industries, Inc.
2081 S. 56th St.
West Allis, WI 53219
(C, S/pv, i)

Syroco
P.O. Box 4875
Syracuse, NY 13202
(SP/p)

Taylor & Ng
1212B 19th St.
Oakland, CA 94607
(SP/m, w)

Techline
Marshall Erdman and Assoc., Inc.
5117 University Ave.
Madison, WI 53705
(S, SP/pv)

Triangle Pacific Corp.
P.O. Box 220100
Dallas, TX 75222
(C, S, SO/pv, w)

Westech Cabinets
143 Business Center Dr.
Corona, CA 91720
(S, SO/pv, w)

Wilton/Copco Enterprises
2240 W. 75th St.
Woodridge, IL 60517
(SP/p)

Wood-Hu Kitchens, Inc.
343 Manley St.
West Bridgewater, MA 02379
(C, S, SO/w)

Wood-Mode Cabinetry
Wood Metal Industries
Kreamer, PA 17833
(C, S, SO/pv, w)

XA Cabinet Corp.
19063 Valley View
La Mirada, CA 90638
(C, S/pv, w)

Yorktowne
P.O. Box 231
Red Lion, PA 17356
(S/pv, w)

Index